The Building Blocks
to a
Strong Marriage

A Marriage Manual in Poetry

by
Viola T. Miller

CCB Publishing
British Columbia, Canada

The Building Blocks to a Strong Marriage:
A Marriage Manual in Poetry

Copyright ©2009 by Viola T. Miller
ISBN-13 978-1-926585-23-9
Second Edition

Library and Archives Canada Cataloguing in Publication
Miller, Viola T., 1941-
The building blocks to a strong marriage: a marriage manual in poetry /
written by Viola T. Miller – 2nd ed.
Previously published under title: Marriage from the ground up.
ISBN 978-1-926585-23-9
1. Marriage--Poetry. 2. Interpersonal relations--Poetry.
I. Miller, Viola T., 1941- . Marriage from the group up. II. Title.
PS3613.I463B83 2009   811'.6   C2009-902349-0

Scripture quotations marked NIV are taken from the Holy Bible, New International Version. Copyright ©1973, 1978, 1984 by the International Bible Society. Used by permission of Zondervan Publishing House. All rights reserved.

Scripture quotations marked (NLT) are taken from the Holy Bible, New Living Translation,copyright©1996.Used by permission of Tyndale House Publishers, Inc., Wheaton, Illinois 60189.All rights reserved.

Scriptures marked (Msg) are taken from the Message Bible © 1993, 1994 1995,196, 2000, 2001, 2002. Used by permission of NavPress Publishing Group.

Scriptures marked (TLB) are taken from the Living Bible Copyright © 1971by Tyndale House Publishers, Wheaton, Illinois 60187. All rights reserved.

Scriptures marked (NKJV) are taken from the New King James Version. Copyright 1979, 1980, 1982 by Thomas Nelson, Inc. Used by permission. All rights reserved.

Scripture quotations marked (Amp) are from the Amplified Bible copyright© 1954, 1958, 1965, 1987 by the Lockman Foundation. Used by permission.
Scripture quotations marked (KJV) are taken from the authorized King James Version of the Holy Bible. All rights reserved.

Extreme care has been taken to ensure that all information presented in this book is accurate and up to date at the time of publishing. Neither the author nor the publisher can be held responsible for any errors or omissions. Additionally, neither is any liability assumed for damages resulting from the use of the information contained herein.

All rights reserved. No part of this publication may be reproduced, stored in a retrieval system or transmitted in any form or by any means, electronic, mechanical, photocopying, recording or otherwise without the express written permission of the publisher. Printed in the United States of America and the United Kingdom.

Publisher: CCB Publishing
             British Columbia, Canada
             www.ccbpublishing.com

Contents

Preface viii
Acknowledgments ix
Introduction x

Part One: The Nature of Marriage
The Origin of Marriage 2
Threefold Cord 3
The Concept of Marriage 4
The Honor of Marriage 6

Part Two: Preparation for Marriage
Am I Prepared Mentally? 8
Am I Insecure? 9
Am I Ready for Marriage? 10
Will Envy Hinder Me As A Spouse? 11
Am I Selfish? 12

Part Three: Choosing the Right Mate
Your Dream Mate 15
Don't Be Anxious 17
Examine Your Prospect's Views 19
Taking an Honest Look 20
Abuse Check 21
Is This the Right Choice? 22
Premarital Counseling 23
What Every Woman Needs in a Husband 25
What Every Man Needs in a Wife 27

Part Four: The Beauty of Marriage
The Beauty of the Marriage Vows 30
The Beauty of the Honeymoon 31
Why the Honeymoon Ends 33
How to Preserve the Honeymoon 34

Part Five: Bonding with Each Other
Marriage Is Much More Than… 36
Adjustments to Each Other 37
Don't Try to Change Your Mate 38
Leaving and Cleaving 39
Excluding In-Laws 40
Beware of Deception 42
The Shock of Reality 43
Disagreements Aren't the End 45

Part Six: The Sanctity of Vows
The Seriousness of Adultery 47
What's Behind Flirting? 48
Adultery is Folly 50
Cast Down Imaginations 51
Jealousy Can Be Acceptable 52
Overcoming Temptation 54
Working Through a Fall 56
Unfaithfulness Revealed 57
Coping with Unfaithfulness 59

Part Seven: Establishing a Strong Marriage
Marriage Can Be Wonderful 61
Commitment Is Paramount 62
Get to Know Your Mate 63
Prayer Is Essential 65
Wisdom Is the Key 66
Crucial Principles 68
Protecting the Relationship 69
Financial Security 71
Keep Romance Alive 72
The Need for Nurturing 73
Take Time for Each Other 75
Identifying Needs 77
Sex and Spirituality 78
Is My Marriage Divorce Proof? 79
Watch Your Words 81

Understanding Submission 83
Confronting Problems 85

Part Eight: The Power of Love
Love's Character 87
The Humility of Love 88
How a Spouse Communicates Love 89
Love's Behavior 90
Tough Love 92
Love's Forbidden List 93

Part Nine: Examine Yourself as a Spouse
What Kind of Mate Are You? 96
Do I Communicate Well? 98
Do I Nag? 99
Am I Mean? 101
Am I Proud? 102
Am I Truthful? 103
Am I Committed? 104

Part Ten: Conflict Resolutions
Attitude for Resolutions 106
Something's Wrong 108
Hidden Offenses 109
Satan Is to Blame 110
Eating Your Words 111
Resolving Conflicts 112

Part Eleven: For Men Only
(Help for Understanding Your Wife)
Value Your Wife 114
Your Image as a Husband 115
Wives Have Special Needs 116
Free Your Wife 117
From a Wife's Perspective 119
Different Construction 120
The Threat of Loneliness 122
Overcoming Myths 123

Part Twelve: For Men Only (Listen to Your Wife)
Listen and Learn 126
She Feels Neglected 127
Why She Has No Interest 129
Help Her Not to Freeze 130
Identifying What She Likes 131

Part Thirteen: For Women Only
(Help for Understanding Your Husband)
Your Image as a Wife 133
Stop Complaining 134
Cut the Chatter 135
Be Informed About Men 136
Understanding Men 137
Communication Relieves Frustration 138

Part Fourteen: For Women Only (Listen to Your Husband)
Give Him Some Space 140
Are You the Cause? 141
Listen More, Talk Less 143
What I Like About You 144

Part Fifteen: Hindrances to a Strong Marriage
Pursuit of Wealth Instead of God 146
Strife Destroys 147
Controlling Anger 148
Fear Weakens Relationships 149
Plea Against Stubbornness 150
Unforgiveness Blocks 151
Unwise Phrases 152

Part Sixteen: Abuse Revealed
Recognizing Abuse 154
Am I Abusive? 155
Submission Myths 156
Coping with Low Self-Esteem 158

Part Seventeen: Dealing with Unsaved Spouses
Place No One Above God 160
Being an Effective Witness 162
Bridging the Gap 163

Part Eighteen: Recognizing Different Seasons in Life
Recognizing the Fear of Aging 166
Changes Will Come 167
Coping with Menopause (Husbands) 168
Coping with Mid-Life Crisis (Wives) 169
Senior Glow 170
Maintaining Loving Focus 171

Part Nineteen: Is There Hope for a Failed Marriage?
Failed Expectations 173
Afterthought 175
It's Not Too Late 176
Overcoming Boredom 177

Part Twenty: Overcoming Defeat
Prayer of Desperation 180
Struggles with Defeat 181
The Last Straw 183
Be Encouraged 185
Decide to be Happy 186
Salvation Commitment 187

About the Author 189

Final Word 191

Preface

Because we live in a microwave society, few people are willing to be patient in working out a solution to problems that arise. If an item doesn't work immediately, the first time, every time, we'll take it back and get another one or a better one. Unfortunately the same has become true of marriages.

Many couples are merely tolerating each other in marriage, and have come to accept that as normal for couples who have been married for a period of time. In most wedding vows, couples promise to love and honor each other for their entire lives. To me, that doesn't mean tolerance; instead, it implies that the one loved is on your mind and in your heart, causing you to constantly seek ways to express that love.

Generally, we are quick to say what we desire in a mate, but few spouses ever check themselves to see how they measure up as a mate.

There is an abundance of helpful information in this manual. The issues addressed span from such concerns of singles as, Readiness for Marriage and Choosing the Right Mate, to Abuse and Unfaithfulness. There are Help-for-Men sections, which will aid in the understanding of wives and their peculiarities; also, Help-For-Women sections for wives will help them to understand the complexities of their husbands. The wisdom that's presented can cause a couple to maintain their separate identities and yet be able to flow together in love and respect for each other.

This book will be a voice which speaks tenderly and clearly enough for every husband or wife to hear, identify, understand and meet each other's needs.

Even though it was primarily written as a means of support, encouragement and enrichment for married couples, it can also be a resource for singles, who are in the process of planning marriage or who are contemplating it in the future.

Be sure to read the scriptural references preceding each part.

Acknowledgements

I am grateful, first of all, to the Lord Jesus Christ for His sustaining strength and unfailing love, in directing my path as this book was written.

I appreciate my husband, Billy, for all the hours he helped me immensely through his spiritual insight, contributions and corrections. His love, patience, encouragement and prayer support have been there to sustain me in persevering to the completion of this project. Thanks, Sweetie.

I would like to thank a longtime friend, Alma Holt, who began urging me to write this book over twenty years ago.

Also, I dedicate this book to our sons and their wives:
Billy & Gwen; Adrian & Shasha

My mentorees:
Joanna, Tracie, Sherita, and Tina

Our promoter/agents:
Kenny& Ella; Dorothy & Elbert
Edna & Ann; Sandra & Mike; Linda & Linzell; Zetta & Stephanie;
Rosie & Althea; Belinda & Christian World

Introduction

Married life can be wonderful, but don't be deceived by anyone who says it will happen as long as: both of you love each other; both of you are financially secure; both of you have the same or similar interests; both of you have similar backgrounds; both of you are Christians and have the same or similar religious affiliations, the same personalities, the same or similar goals in life, or any other thing one could name. Any one or all of the above may play a small part, but there is nothing short of hard work, much prayer, a total dependency on God, perseverance, a willingness to learn, a willingness to unlearn, an unwavering determination and willingness to compromise, that will come close to producing the marriage one desires.

Our marriage isn't perfect by any stretch of the imagination, but we are enjoying a wonderful relationship after more than four decades. Even though we've come to know each other, faults and all, we're still actively in love and enjoying a wonderful life together.

When I first got married, I was told that the first year or two would be the best years of marriage, then, it would only be routine and regret. Today, I am thankful that when I heard those words, they broke my heart and I was determined to prove them wrong; by the grace of God, I have done so.

I believe the keys to our success have been our sincere love for each other, our faith in God, and our unwavering commitment to build and live our marriage by the principles of God's Word. With that being so, Bible study, prayer, communication, honor for one another and time with each other are high priorities in our home. Divorce has never been an option for us; therefore, we've been committed to conflict resolution in order to live happy, fulfilled lives.

In writing this book I have drawn from scriptural insight and inspiration, our personal experiences, as well as, from the successes and mistakes I've observed in other marriages, in their varying degrees of development or destruction.

I believe that it is rare to find a book on marriage, written entirely in poetic form.

It is my prayer that the information will glorify God as it convicts, encourages, inspires, restores, challenges, enriches, or serves in any other way that is helpful to the readers.

VTM

Part One

The Nature of Marriage

And the Lord said, "It is not good for man to be alone; I will make a companion for him, a helper suited to his needs." (Genesis 2:18, TLB)

So the Lord God caused Adam to fall into a deep sleep. He took one of his ribs and closed up the place from which he had taken it. Then the Lord God made a woman from the rib and brought her to Adam. This explains why a man leaves his father and mother and is joined to his wife, and the two are united into one. (Genesis 2: 21, 22, 24, 25, NLT)

…It's good for a man to have a wife, and for a woman to have a husband. Sexual drives are strong, but marriage is strong enough to contain them and provide for a balanced and fulfilling sexual life in a world of sexual disorder. (I Corinthians 7:2, Msg)

Do nothing out of selfish ambition or vain conceit, but in humility, consider others better than yourselves. Each of you should look not only to your own interests, but also to the interest of others. (Philippians 2:3, 4, NIV)

The Building Blocks to a Strong Marriage

The Origin of Marriage

When the first marriage was made,
Was its claim then set?
What purpose was it to fill,
And has that claim been met?

For whom was it meant?
And how was it to be?
Would it be for earth only,
Or for all eternity?

The God of all creation
Who made the human race,
Knew from the beginning
This was something we'd face.

When Adam named the animals
And he saw their counterpart,
Loneliness was then born,
Conceived within his heart.

Being aware of his condition,
And the lack within man,
God, in his wise council
Conceived for him a plan.

After causing man to sleep,
He then lovingly proceeded,
As He took from his side
To make what he needed.

What he made was breathtaking,
The loveliest of all creatures,
The epitome of beauty
With all gorgeous features.

Together they began a journey
To enjoy a fulfilled life,
Without a care in the world
United as husband and wife.

With such a perfect setting,
What could possibly go wrong?
What could possibly cause trouble,
To mar such a happy home?

The Serpent did it then
Pretending to be a friend,
And he's still wholly committed
To causing marriages to end.

Viola T. Miller

Threefold Cord

The first marriage began with God,
And all others should too.
Then the threefold cord
Would be hard to break through.

A couple may seem compatible,
And all may appear to be well,
But if God's not in the relationship,
It will eventually fail.

When marriage was created,
Three formed the original cord.
The husband and wife were joined
And God was indeed their Lord.

The union was to remain in place,
Cemented by what Adam heard;
They were united in matrimony,
By God's spoken word.

God chose the perfect woman
To fill Adam's lack in life;
For only by His hands,
Could he have a prudent wife.

God should never be left out
As one goes on his/her own,
To seek that life-time mate
On human wisdom alone.

The choice will not be wise,
Neither the foundation sure,
Because without the threefold cord
The marriage won't be secure.

God placed Himself in marriage
And when He's kept in the equation,
The marriage is insulated
Against demonic persuasion.

Leaning to earthly understanding,
Wisdom can easily fade fast;
But with the threefold cord,
Whatever is built will last.

God is the all sufficient one
To get one perfectly matched,
And by following His rules,
Couples aren't easily detached.

The Concept of Marriage

Many have entered marriage
And found themselves deceived,
Because of misconceptions
Or false information received.

The concept of marriage
Has undergone much it seems;
Through many years of history
It's changed in what it means.

Some have entered into it
With the wrong reason in mind,
And have abandoned it quickly
When it they could not find.

Since God is the author of marriage
And He has revealed His mind
It is only by Him
That it is correctly defined.

It's a man and woman's declaration
As themselves they give,
In commitment to each other
As long as they shall live.

It is a promise of love
Which both enter into,
To be enjoyed exclusively
For all their lives through.

It is a pledge of unity
To always be in place,
To cleave to each other
Whatever each may face.

Viola T. Miller

It is a total commitment
Which by a covenant is sealed
And it remains in force
According to the couple's will.

The Honor of Marriage

Marriage is an honorable thing,
And it is to be desired.
Those who master its secret
Are to be admired.

For its health and success,
The Bible has much to say,
As it reveals the light
That unfolds its way.

When love draws two together,
And they decide to wed,
A cocoon is then established
And formal vows are said.

God bestows His favor,
As He blesses their way.
Yet their journey to unity
Is challenged day by day.

It is only by perversions
And not receiving what's right,
That marriages have suffered
And often lacked delight.

It is to be a relationship
With ample nourishment and love,
Having abundant joy and favor
Supplied from God above.

It is to be uncommonly
 harmonious,
Where there's mutual satisfaction,
With no outside interference
Or any adulterous action.

It is to never to be slain
When problems against it assail,
For being built upon the rock,
By love it will not fail.

Christ's own revelation
Symbolizing Him and His bride,
Is epitomized by marriage
Unless it fails through pride.

Even if it fails,
Again, it can live
When both partners recommit
Of themselves to give.

It is a promise of exclusion
To let no others in,
But to be faithful
And give no place to sin.

This pledge of eternal loyalty
Is never to be broken,
And it's never to be treated
As if empty words spoken.

Though it may fall far short
Of God's intended ideal,
It is still a possibility
By adherers to His will.

Part Two

Preparation for Marriage

The preparations of the heart in man and the answer of the tongue is from the Lord.

All the ways of a man are clean in his own eyes, but the Lord weighs the spirits. (Proverbs 16:1, 2, NLT)

How can I know all the sins lurking in my heart? Cleanse me from the hidden faults.

Search me, O God, and know my heart; test me and know my anxious thoughts.

Put me on trial Lord, and cross-examine me. Test my motives and affections. (Psalms 19:12; Psalms 139:23; Psalms 26:2, NLT)

... But if they cannot control themselves, they should marry, for it is better to marry than to burn with passion. (I Corinthians 7:9, NIV)

The Building Blocks to a Strong Marriage

Am I Prepared Mentally?

Preparation takes time
If all is to be searched out,
For one cannot very easily
Move away from doubt.

Am I prepared in every way
For the journey I plan to take?
Am I truly ready now
For changes I must make?

Am I willing to admit ignorance
And learn what I don't know?
Would I be willing to move,
 If my spouse had to go?

Am I prepared to share
And not call things my own?
Am I willing to adjust
And not please myself alone?

Am I prepared mentally,
To begin thinking in two's?
Does it cause concern
That my singleness I'll lose?

Am I already prepared
To submit as a husband or wife,
With no longer exclusive control
Over what happens in my life?

Am I prepared financially,
Or do I have farther to go?
Should I wait a while
Until I'm certain that I know?

Do my answers indicate to me
That I should go ahead?
Or do they tell me emphatically,
That I should wait instead?

Hesitations mean uncertainty,
And perhaps I still should wait.
It could mean take more time
Before I set my date.

I need to consider this seriously
And really pray about it too,
Because everything should be settled
Prior to my saying "I do."

Viola T. Miller

Am I Insecure?

Do I become troubled,
When others are improved?
Do I fear my superiority
By others will be removed?

Do I have insecurity
Though it's subtly tucked away?
Do I reject good ideas
Because I will not sway?

If others have suggestions
When I have the floor,
Do I refuse to yield,
Fearing they might know more?

Do I hate group work,
Since it gives me no light
And because combined credit
Edges me out of sight?

If this is true of me
I know the reason why;
I need help with insecurity
And that I can't deny.

This is extra baggage
I must rid myself of,
Or I'll have difficulty
Receiving another's love.

And neither will I securely
Be able to give it out,
For all along the way
I'll fight myself with doubt.

The answers to my questions
Reveal what I should do,
Whether I should marry
Or decide not to.

I ask help for myself
As I seek God's face,
May He lead my decision
By His divine grace.

The Building Blocks to a Strong Marriage

Am I Ready for Marriage?

Am I a whole person now,
Or do I hope to be complete?
Am I expecting it will happen
Through some dream-person I'll meet?

What do I have to offer?
How would I be as a mate?
I need to know these answers
As marriage I contemplate.

Am I ready for marriage?
Ready to share what I own?
Can I pledge my allegiance
To one person alone?

Do I value my independence
And flaunt it for all to see?
Am I a self-willed person
With no compromise in me?

Could I be under subjection,
Or have my desires denied?
How important is it to me
That I am satisfied?

Do I find it very difficult
To work through a test?
When my help is needed,
Do I do my very best?

Do I hold grudges
And refuse to forgive?
Am I a pleasant person
With whom to live?

Do I have any hurts
Still alive in my mind?
Some things I can't get over
And I can't leave them behind?

How big is my world?
Does it have room for another?
Is there only space for me,
With no room for any other?

I must think before answering,
And then make up my mind.
My state after consideration
Will reveal if I need time.

Viola T. Miller

Will Envy Hinder Me as a Spouse?

Envy is like a cancer,
Because it eats away at you;
It poisons your whole system
And everything you do.

It affects one's health,
Right down to the bones
And it's the silent killer
That seeks to wreck all homes.

As I prepare for marriage,
And the part that I must play,
I examine my heart for envy
So it won't block my way.

When someone does something
That I know was good,
Do I acknowledge it joyfully,
As I know I should?

Do I feel any uneasiness
If someone does well?
Do I feel any regret
If I hear they've failed?

Does another person's success
Which seems better than mine,
Often rob me of peace
For a period of time?

Do I work diligently
To make a project go?
When I cause its success
Must every one around know?

If some one else's performance
Is better than what I do,
Does frustration overwhelm me
And cause me to be blue?

Do I ever withhold info
Or try to keep it down
And hope by doing so,
It will not be found?

Have I hidden these secrets
And hoped they wouldn't show?
Have I been deceived,
Thinking even God doesn't know?

If these emotional conditions
Seem prevalent in my life,
They show I'm not ready yet
To become a husband or wife.

In a marriage relationship
Envy should have no place,
For teamwork is paramount
And should cover every space.

Am I Selfish?

How is selfishness defined,
Or what does it mean?
Can it by other people
In me be easily seen?

Selfishness is to be concerned
About myself and no other.
It is not being sensitive
About conditions of another.

It is thoughts of me only
And just letting others be.
As long as I'm taken care of
That's all that counts with me.

Because of self-centeredness
Only my desires fill my mind,
And meeting others' needs
Is a path that's hard to find.

Selfishness is being sure for myself,
That I stay ahead.
It's not sharing my means
But hoarding them up instead.

It's doing what I like
And not considering any around;
It's demanding others' support,
Yet none from me is found.

If I have this attitude
And it's found in common occurrence,
Then I must overcome it
And embrace instead deference.

Viola T. Miller

It may require giving up demands
Of having to receive first choice
Or being quiet sometimes
And allowing my mate a voice.

But the first step is recognition
When something is going on wrong,
And the next is willingness to stop it
And not allow it to go on.

Part Three

Choosing the Right Mate

Houses and land are handed down from parents, but a congenial spouse comes from the Lord. (Proverbs 19:14, Msg)

The man who finds a wife finds a good thing; she is a blessing to him from the Lord.

If you find a truly good wife, she is worth more than precious gems! She is a woman of strength and dignity and has no fear of old age. When she speaks her words are wise, and kindness is the rule of everything she says. She watches carefully all that goes on throughout her household and is never lazy. (Proverbs 18:22; 31:10, 25-27; TLB)

Viola T. Miller

Your Dream Mate

Your eyes can hardly sleep
And you seldom want to eat;
And when you think of him/her
Your heart skips a beat.

He/she is always on your mind
Or at least that's how it seems.
When you fall asleep
This person is in your dreams.

Ah! To share a lifetime together-
This is your greatest aim,
For you know what you feel
Will always be the same.

You feel this person is ideal,
And all about him/her is right.
This, you know is true
Since your love was at first sight.

Have you checked all things out?
Are there any doubts this is real?
Could anything change your mind
So that you wouldn't go on still?

There could be something-
Perhaps a question you should ask,
Before you begin to embark
Upon this lifetime task.

So engage yourself a few moments,
By giving reasoning a place.
Then you may proceed
From whatever challenge you face.

The Building Blocks to a Strong Marriage

You have nothing to lose
But you've much to gain.
Afterwards continue onward,
If all remains the same.

Viola T. Miller

Don't Be Anxious

You may feel a bit anxious,
Thinking life's passing you by.
With all that you have to offer,
You constantly wonder why.

Don't sell yourself short,
Thinking there is no hope
Therefore, you accept someone
Who is already on dope.

Thinking a person will change,
Only means you're deceived.
Against your better judgment,
This lie you've believed.

If you're feeling pressured
As you seek for a woman or man,
Don't mistakenly settle
For someone unable to stand.

Entering with a plan "B"
May seem to be sound,
But a relationship like this
Will not get off the ground.

The only way out
Is to never get into it,
For there's no forcing
Two different shapes to fit.

Quiet your anxious thoughts,
And set your priorities straight.
Unless character is obvious
Indeed, you really should wait.

The Building Blocks to a Strong Marriage

> Ask God for help
> And He'll reveal what's true
> Then you can avoid problems
> That would devastate you.

Viola T. Miller

Examine Your Prospect's Views

A person may seem to be right,
But yet he/she must be checked out.
For all things must be discussed
To take away all doubt.

Everything should be examined,
And brought to open view.
For anything that's assumed,
May return to haunt you.

Religious views must be checked
To see how they compare.
Though convictions can be respected,
They must be sifted through prayer.

Nothing should be brushed off
As though it doesn't count.
For that same issue later,
May become paramount.

All questions must be settled
Concerning the family plan,
And all must be discussed
As each declares his stand.

All matters must be addressed
Before plans are set.
If there's unresolved disagreement,
Marriage could be a regret.

Financial views are primary,
For they can cause much stress.
And from their unresolved conflict,
The marriage will suffer unrest.

To trust in a surface relationship
Is certainly not very wise,
Though all may seem well
And compatible in your eyes.

God sees beyond the physical,
And He knows things we don't.
Unless we look to Him
We may get something we don't want.

He declares of Himself
He already knows the end,
And He'll reveal it to us
Before we ever begin.

So to get the right life partner,
We should listen to His voice,
And He'll direct our path
To help us make the best choice.

Taking an Honest Look

As I examined this person,
What did I find?
Were there any cautions
That entered into my mind?

Have questions arisen
Since we have met,
Which caused me to be uneasy
And just a bit upset?

Have I seen or heard anything
Which I wish I hadn't seen?
Has there been anything revealed
That says this person is mean?

Do we often argue,
Having negative conversations,
And from them we separate
Due to harsh frustrations?

Am I settling for this person,
Hoping marriage will make me whole?
Am I desperate for a mate
Because I am getting old?

Am I in denial ,
Because I choose to be?

Have I turned my head,
Away from what I see?

Am I deliberately ignoring
What I should give attention?
Am I keeping quiet
On something I should mention?

If my answers are troubling,
I really need to pray.
I shouldn't move onward
And be married anyway.

Peace is the indicator
That everything is all right,
After carefully exposing
All things to the light.

If peace is present
After all is said and done,
Then it could be God saying
That this is the right one.

He knows everything,
And He knows everybody too.
So I look to Him for guidance
Before saying "I do."

Viola T. Miller

Abuse Check

Is this person too fast,
Pushing me too hard,
Pressing me for a decision
Before I know my heart.

Do I see something suspicious,
A behavior I can't stand,
Yet I just overlook it,
Hoping this is the right man?

Do I hear a controlling voice
When he makes demands?
Does he ignore my suggestions,
While he makes all the plans?

When I disagree with him,
Does he claim to be mistreated?
When I give in to him,
Do I feel that I'm defeated?

Do I feel uneasy
When he comes to my home?
Do I feel unprotected
When we are alone?

Does he appear to be all hands
With nothing in his head?
Is he interested in going anywhere
Except to the bed?

Is he too close for comfort
And refuses to move back?
Do I feel I'm being threatened,
As though under attack?

Is this person possessive?
Does he/she push or shove?
Have I ever been grabbed harshly,
And it was labeled love?

These are warning signs,
That are primers to abuse.
They are intolerable behavior
And are without excuse.

With this conscious
  acknowledgment,
It would be foolish to go ahead.
I should reevaluate the source
And place all on hold instead.

Is This the Right Choice?

Before it's set in stone,
While all is temporary,
Check what might surface
That could prove to be contrary.

What is the first test
That your prospect must pass,
In order to be assured
That the relationship will last?

Does this person know God?
Is he/she really true?
Or is it just performance
In order to marry you?

If he/she doesn't know Him,
All good will fade fast,
And what seems right now
Won't be able to last.

How long have you known each
  other?
So far, what have you been shown?
Have there been enough occasions
So true character could be known?

If you've only been acquainted
For a very short while,

Then you don't know very much
About his or her lifestyle.

Short term courtships
Will not be very revealing,
For there's no time to expose
What one might be concealing.

Is he/she boastful or proud
Or perhaps overly pessimistic?
When evaluating this person
Are you being realistic?

Is there a change of voice tone,
When you don't comply?
Does another person emerge
When you are demanded "why?"

Honestly ask yourself these
  questions
And to your own self be true.
See if your answers are satisfactory
Or, are they puzzling to you?

Can you spend with this person
The rest of your days?
Or, after close examination,
Should you go your separate ways?

Viola T. Miller

Premarital Counseling

Premarital counseling is helpful,
For it exposes issues of doubt.
It can settle potential problems,
That may be hiding out.

Some things not thought of
Could prove to be a test.
But if they're dealt with properly,
They can be laid to rest.

Even though love is sure,
Challenges occur just the same,
Especially if an "ex"
Already wears your name.

If there are previous children,
Who're out of the picture now,
They may emerge from obscurity
After you've said your vow.

If there're outstanding debts,
They'll affect both of you.
For previous responsibilities
Must be considered too.

What about child support?
How long will it last?
Can it be accepted
Without resentment over the past?

How will you handle finances,
So that both are satisfied?

Are there any annoyances
That either attempts to hide?

Discussions must be thorough,
And agreements must be made;
Otherwise, a sure foundation
Never can really be laid.

If you have likes or dislikes,
Things you can't tolerate,
A counselor can help you face
  them
And work with you and your mate.

How you roll your tissue,
Or how you squeeze tooth paste,
May become an issue
Or problems you must face.

Money matters and working,
Saving and spending too,
Will be placed on the table
When someone counsels you.

Whether you want children
Or pets you can't stand,
If these aren't addressed,
They may get out of hand.

Whether it's taking out garbage
Or cleaning up the house,
It' pays to know the position
Of your potential spouse.

The Building Blocks to a Strong Marriage

A counselor helps each discover
What neither may not know,
And determine if you're willing
To compromise and grow.

By facing different aspects
Of each other's life,
A couple is more prepared
To adjust as a husband or wife.

Viola T. Miller

What Every Woman Needs in a Husband

Every woman needs protection
By a husband that's strong;
She needs one she trusts
To help her build a home.

She needs his confidence
That she is genuinely loved,
And is not replaceable,
But most highly thought of.

One who can be looked up to
Whenever things go wrong,
One who will be there
Whenever she needs him home.

One who is not possessive,
But allows her to be free;
One she's proud she married
And wants everyone to see.

She needs one who is considerate,
Desiring the best for her life,
One who is not selfish
In providing for his wife.

She needs to have a husband
Who takes pride in family care,
And one who is a willing partner,
Who stands with her in prayer.

She needs a role model,
One her children can emulate,
One who commands their respect,
Yet with them participate.

She needs a faithful husband,
Who keeps his commitment pure;
One who unconditionally loves her
And sees that she's secure.

She needs an attractive husband,
Who takes pride in his appearance;
One she esteems highly
And allows no interference.

She needs one who appreciates her,
For being the joy of his life,
One who considers her
The world's greatest wife.

She needs to feel attractive
To the man who shares her bed,
And not always be told by others
What her husband should have said.

She needs affection consistently
By loving touches and deeds,
From a husband who is patient
And fills her sexual needs.

She needs a husband to follow,
Feeling no need to lead,
Because he is insecure
And satisfied not to succeed.

The Building Blocks to a Strong Marriage

One who is conscientious
And constantly ready to move,
One who is business-minded
And ever seeking to improve.

If the person in question,
These traits seem to carry,

It may be God's leading
That he's the one to marry.

Both need to trust Him
For the final decision
Because He knows all things
And will give divine vision.

Viola T. Miller

What Every Man Needs in a Wife

A man needs to feel appreciated
And be held in high esteem,
By a wife who stands with him
And helps him achieve his dream.

He needs to feel trusted
To take care of what's wrong,
And he desires in everything
To be perceived strong.

He doesn't need pressure
Because of constant unrest,
Stemming from accusations,
Though he is doing his best.

He needs honor and admiration
And to feel respected.
And his position as head
Should always be protected.

He needs to be assured
He can trust his wife anywhere,
And whenever he needs her
She'll try her best to be there.

He needs his wife as confidante,
Who won't his secrets share,
Nor divulge information
Thinking he won't care.

He needs sexual fulfillment
Without a lot of frustration,
And to have a willing wife
With enthusiastic participation.

He needs an attractive wife
Who is cheerful and smart,
One who makes him proud
And loves him with all her heart.

He needs a wife who is peaceful,
One who is kind and sweet,
One who is intelligent
And who is organized and neat.

He needs a wife who is considerate
And looks after her home,
One who possesses many virtues
Which serve to make her strong.

He needs a wife who loves her children,
But keeps them in line,
Not allowing them to manipulate
And control all of her time.

He needs a wife, who is honest,
Who only speaks what is true,
And imparts these character traits
Into her children too.

He needs a praying wife,
Who'll help him to move along,
One who will speak up
And not go along with wrong.

The Building Blocks to a Strong Marriage

He needs a committed wife,
Though he may not be so;
For then she can help him
To find God's purpose and grow.

If the woman in question
Possesses these qualities of life,

Then your heart may be saying
This should be your wife.

In everything that you do
Trust that God will be there,
Then He'll impart to you wisdom,
Whenever you meet Him in
   prayer.

Part Four

The Beauty of Marriage

You have ravished my heart, my lovely one, my bride; I am overcome by one glance of your eyes …

How sweet is your love, my darling, my bride. How much better is it than mere wine. The perfume of your love is more fragrant than all the richest spices.

My darling bride is like a private garden, a spring that no one else can have, a fountain of my own.

Many waters cannot quench the flame of love; neither can the floods drown it. If a man tried to buy it with everything he owned, he couldn't do it. (Song of Solomon 4:9, 10, 12; 8:12, TLB)

The Beauty of the Marriage Vows

A man and woman come together
To share each other's life;
They come to experience the blessings
Of being husband and wife.

They leave father and mother
That together they may cleave,
And never depend again
Upon those whom they leave.

They establish a covenant
Before God and man,
To forever be united
And together always stand.

As a symbol of their union
Each gives to the other a ring,
Both vowing until death
To share their everything.

They express pledges of love
And without any reservations,
They promise to be faithful
In all their situations.

She promises him her allegiance,
To love honor and obey,
And to remain forever loyal
Whatever might come their way.

His promise is to love and cherish her
As long as they both shall live,
And he pledges to no other
His love he shall give.

Together they join hands
As they bow down in prayer,
And both call upon God
That He'd always be there.

Then the minister signals,
And gives the kiss- command;
The vows are then sealed,
Witnessed by God and man.

Their search has now ended
And their joy that's awaited,
Finds completion and fulfillment
As the marriage is consummated.

Viola T. Miller

The Beauty of the Honeymoon

The honeymoon commences
When marriage vows are said,
And all is joy and laughter
For the ones who are wed.

The attention is majestic,
And passion is unashamed;
Responses are spontaneous
And rejection is never named.

Deference is primary
And "self" is off the throne;
The other partner is important,
And constantly he/she is shown.

Time is of no essence,
And nothing seems unfair.
Much effort is employed
That each is always there.

Each makes himself available
And does his very best,
In avoiding situations
That might become a test.

Little effort is required
To respond in a kind voice,
As each competes with the other
To give him the first choice.

Attitudes are always pleasant,
Agreement and approval are
  sought,
Neither seeks to ridicule
Or expose the other's fault.

Each is anxious to please,
As the other is admired;
Differences aren't annoyances,
And conformity is not required.

Peace and harmony flow
And selfishness has no place,
Neither complains of being
  needed
Or demands one's own space.

Communication is not strenuous,
Words seem to abound,
Loving thoughts preserve
  closeness
When the other isn't around.

Help needs no soliciting,
Courtesy is on display,
Appreciation for each other
Is employed day by day.

Although needs are different
Neither one will complain,
And no impatience is voiced
Because paces aren't the same.

One is a morning person,
The other prefers the night
But nothing is rejected
Because anytime is all right.

The Building Blocks to a Strong Marriage

Each just makes adjustments
And never appears annoyed
But provides for the allowance
So harmony won't be destroyed.

How wonderful it is on earth
To have such beautiful lives
And to share them so sublimely
As blessed husbands and wives.

It would be more wonderful
If both remembered their vow,
Then troubles would be worked out
And the honeymoon would last
  somehow.

Viola T. Miller

Why the Honeymoon Ends

Why does it have to fade?
Why must it leave?
What happens to the promise,
That each would always cleave?

It doesn't happen suddenly,
But gradually finds ways,
By something one does,
Or something one says.

A thought goes unchecked,
Or one is tempted or stressed,
One doesn't share feelings,
And wrongs are not confessed.

Negatives increase more and more
Until nothing seems the same,
Then hearts become calloused
And next there's blame.

Before accusations are spoken
They're conceived in the mind,
That's a truth that's hidden
But it is easy to find.

How does a couple get there?
What is each one's part?
The answer to the question
Is found in their heart.

At some point or time
Wrong feelings will come,
But don't entertain them
For you know where they're from.

Unchecked thoughts are serious
Though only a seed
But when they aren't cancelled,
They become a deed.

No one remembers getting off,
Or each is too proud to say;
But both play some part
In the marriage going astray.

The Building Blocks to a Strong Marriage

How to Preserve the Honeymoon

There must be a way
For it was meant to last,
Why should something come in
That makes the honeymoon pass.

Diligence must be constant
And never left behind.
Awareness must be engaged
And always easy to find.

Each spouse must keep in mind
The attraction from the start,
And keep it in active pursuit,
Ever alive in the heart.

Each must note special days
And be faithful to celebrate.
Keep them stamped
  "important"
And schedule for each a date.

But days need not be special
For one to make them such
Because the element of surprise
Profits relationships much.

The willingness to continue
When ease and passions aren't
  there
Requires decision and
  commitment
And seeking help through prayer.

God is there to aid us
Because to Him we belong
And He delightfully reveals
How marriages can stay strong.

In giving we'll receive,
In sowing we will reap
And all who trust in Him,
He will uphold and keep.

Marriage was God's idea
And everything He made was
  right.
He will not change His mind
Because of a couple's fight.

He foreknew all about spats,
And that's why He made
  provision,
By supplying both with
  forgiveness,
To be activated by a decision.

To experience a lasting
  honeymoon,
It won't be an easy road,
But it'll require willingness
To share each other's load.

Finally, neither should be selfish,
Demanding one's way by force.
Instead, willingly compromise
To keep the marriage on course.

Part Five

Bonding with Each Other

Therefore shall a man leave his father and mother and cleave to his wife: And they shall be one flesh.
And they were both naked, the man and his wife, and they were not ashamed. (Genesis 2:24, 25 KJV)

...My son-be faithful and true to your wife.
Be happy, yes rejoice in the wife of your youth. (Proverbs 5:18)

...and let the wife see that she respects and reverences her husband-that she notices him, regards him, honors him, prefers him, venerates him, and esteems him; and that she defers to him, praises him, and loves and admires him exceedingly. (Ephesians 5:33b, AMP)

The husband should not deprive his wife of sexual intimacy, which is her right as a married woman, nor should the wife deprive her husband. (I Corinthians 7:3, NLT)

Marriage Is Much More Than...

Marriage is much more than
All you've thought of.
It's more than any fantasy
One considers love.

It's more than a dream,
Though one must be in mind
But there must be a vision
To stand the test of time.

Marriage is more than
A partnership of duty;
It extends far beyond
A mere ceremony of beauty.

Marriage is much more than
Two just sharing a bed.
It's becoming one together
As together they move ahead.

It is the sharing of yourself
With one whom you trust;
It is unreserved commitment
To doing whatever you must.

It is giving up self-centeredness
And considering your mate.

When there's disagreement,
It's being willing to wait.

It's leaving behind your family
And those considered dear.
It's joining another's purpose
When from God you hear.

Marriage is being willing
With another one to grow;
It is facing the future together
And helping each other flow.

It is helping one another
To discover God's plan.
It is always being there
To give a helping hand.

It is helping each other
To develop into his/her best
As into each other's life
Both willingly invest.

It is a new way of learning
And extending one's all,
As each answers God's
 challenge
To the oneness call.

Viola T. Miller

Adjustments to Each Other

Because you're no longer single,
You must consider another.
Your mate is part of everything
In one way or other.

By deferring to your spouse
You will eventually build a bond,
Then your relationship will develop
As you merge into one.

As your needs become secondary
While your spouse's you attend,
Both will soon discover
It's a process to an end.

As you engage this thinking,
Selfishness will drop from you,
And soon sharing everything
Will be natural for you to do.

Sharing your personal time
And dividing your space,
Will cause a close bonding
To somehow take place.

Single life may've been great
But now it is replaced.
Prepare for the adjustments
That you know must be faced.

You'll need to make allowances
For views that aren't the same,
As you seek together continually
Perfect harmony to gain.

Friction is certain to come
Though you struggle to keep it away,
But as you ask for directions,
God will show you the way.

You cannot be stubborn
But must come to realize,
There'll be many times
That each must compromise.

Things won't always happen
As you wish them to.
But by open communication
All can be worked through.

Remember two are involved
But God wants you one.
So trust Him to work with you
Until He is done.

Your problems may be real,
But they're not too hard;
God has joined you together
So let nothing pull you apart.

The Building Blocks to a Strong Marriage

Don't Try to Change Your Mate

Don't try changing each other;
It'll only prove disaster.
By seeking a blending together,
A change will come much faster.

Endeavoring to duplicate yourself
Is selfishness in disguise.
But appreciating your differences
Will prove indeed to be wise.

It is not a requirement
That a couple becomes the same,
Before their functional unity,
The two of them can claim.

Both can be opposites,
Yet each can be complete,
And neither has to experience
Any deficiency or defeat.

If preferences are different,
Why should they threaten one
  another?
Both of you can be free,
As you complement each other.

Help each other to excel
In your respective roles,
Without causing undue pressure
As each one's dream unfolds.

Both should be sensitive
While seeking accommodation,
And as much as possible,
Engage no hesitation.

Because of unselfish love
And the care that both feel,
Neither should insist on
  something
Which is against the other's will.

What one enjoys as a hobby,
May the other seek to relate,
Then by unselfish support
Both can celebrate.

Let there be no resentment,
No envy and no strife,
And let there be no undermining
By either husband or wife,

When one achieves something,
Let both together share,
And if there be any failure,
Be sure that support is there.

Viola T. Miller

Leaving and Cleaving

Whatever your past relationships
Consider them now dead,
Then your spirit, soul and body
Can focus on ahead.

Anything or anyone known
Who could possibly divide,
Should no longer be allowed
But must be laid aside.

Whatever influenced the past,
Let both willingly leave,
Only embrace the present
And to each other cleave.

Rid yourself of reminders.
They will only cloud your way,
Then they'll claim your attention
And will slowly cause decay.

Rehearse no fond memories,
Nor give bad ones a place.
There are enough things to think of
In the relationship you face.

Don't allow your past mistakes
To influence your present day.
Don't use them to judge your spouse
In some unfair way.

Never cause any suspicion
On a past situation,
By insensitive remarks
Or unsolicited information.

Children from former relationships
Will have their permanent connection,
But keep your side structured
For your own protection.

God will give you wisdom and help,
If invited into your situations,
Then anything can be overcome
In your present relations.

Excluding In-Laws

Let your home reflect you two
And not your mom and dad.
Don't let your contentment
Be based on what they had.

Neither one should ever mention
That present life is inferior
Because your life back home
Was so much superior.

Let this never be permitted,
For it only causes friction.
Make the comparison of in- laws
Be an off- limits' restriction.

When decisions are made,
They should be the couple's choice.
Outsiders should have no vote
Unless both give them voice.

A couple should function independently,
Making boundaries for others known.
All their problems should be solved,
By God and them alone.

When either discloses to parents
All their concerns and cares,
Unconsciously, permission is given
To control intimate affairs,

Always consider each other
And not allow privacy invasion.
Never give Satan a place
By yielding to his persuasion.

Viola T. Miller

When two people are united,
Only God is to be included.
Others are to be kept out
And be forever excluded.

Beware of Deception

Deception is a separator,
And it's easy to fall into,
Especially for those unacquainted
With schemes Satan tries on you.

Everyone is vulnerable
So no one is exempted,
Since we have an enemy
Desiring that all be tempted.

He's looking for an entrance
Into an unprotected heart;
He seeks to sever relationships
And cause couples to part.

Anyone is his candidate
As he seeks to ruin a life,
But his task is impossible
Unless he finds some strife.

He works through suggestions
But sometimes he's bold.
Before one realizes it,
Some secret he'll unfold.

A word may not be voiced
But unrest begins to brew,
And before either is aware
A pit you've fallen into.

At the moment of detection
Let it no longer proceed.
Call out for God's help,
And He'll deliver indeed.

Viola T. Miller

The Shock of Reality

Reality will surely hit
Though you don't think so.
So you're totally shocked
Whenever it does show.

When it becomes blatant,
And you can no longer ignore,
You may begin to wonder
What's different than before.

Nothing really has changed
It is as it's always been,
But reality just surfaced
From somewhere down within.

When your eyes are opened
Then you can take off the
  blinders.
By looking from side to side,
You'll then see all the reminders.

A reminder that life is real
And not a world of make-believe;
A reminder that whatever you sow
That, you will also receive.

There'll be a rude awakening,
All things won't meet your
  expectation;
And from other realizations,
All won't be exhilaration.

Spontaneous reactions will begin
  fading
And effort must be employed.
Whenever it's not chosen,
Much will not be enjoyed.

There'll be the first disagreement
Where each must use restraint,
In order not to blurt out
In the form of a complaint.

There'll be that first negative
  feeling
When there's something you want
  to say
And you find it difficult
To respond in a positive way.

None of these are abnormal
So don't let them get you down,
They are all part of growing
  together
And adjusting to what you've
  found.

Don't allow things to accumulate,
Thinking they'll soon go away.
Nothing just disappears
Without showing up someday.

Because you are different
  individuals,
You naturally have different
  minds.

The Building Blocks to a Strong Marriage

But you can negotiate and blend
The differences each one finds.

So at the first sign of conflict,
Don't dare panic and run;
Many serious adjustments
May very well not be fun.

If you keep God on the
  throne,
And remember He's always there,
He will direct your pathway
If He's met in prayer.

Viola T. Miller

Disagreements Aren't the End

When a couple disagrees,
It may seem that all is gone.
One or both may withdraw
And may feel he/she's alone.

There may be feelings of
  desertion
And it may seem all is lost;
Restoration may appear unlikely,
Because it comes at a high cost.

Honestly examine your heart
And give your spouse a chance.
You initiate reconciliation
And refuse an unyielding stance.

If you are the one at fault,
Don't try to point your finger.
It'll only prolong separation
And cause the problem to linger.

Your confession of a wrong
Doesn't mean your partner has
  won,
But it shows your strength of
  character
Because of what's being done.

Respect is built unconsciously
When humility is found in you;
Then trust will be increased
In other things you do.

By showing yourself cordial
And not willing to hold a grudge,
You can promote restoration
With just a gentle nudge.

Constantly pressing your point
Because you think you're right,
Might win for you an argument,
But still you lose the fight.

There are no winners in
  arguments,
When a home is filled with strife,
So it's better to lose a few
To promote peace in your life.

There're no magic solutions
That'll fix every situation,
But with every problem
There is a road to reconciliation.

Being able to find it,
No matter what you face,
Is the piece of the puzzle
That holds things in place.

Part Six

The Sanctity of Vows

You were united to your wife by the Lord. In God's wise plan, when you married, the two of you became one person in His sight. And what does He want? Godly children from your union. Therefore, guard your passions! Keep faith with the wife of your youth. (Malachi 2:15, TLB)

Run from anything that gives you the evil thoughts...but stay close to anything that makes you want to do right. (II Timothy 2:22, TLB)

Marriage is honorable in all, and the bed undefiled but whoremongers and adulterers God will judge. (Hebrews 13:4, KJV)

You have heard that the Law of Moses says, "Do not commit adultery." But I say anyone who looks at a woman with lust in his eyes has already committed adultery with her in his heart. (Matthew 5:27, NLT)

Viola T. Miller

The Seriousness of Adultery

When you repeat marriage vows,
Standing before God and man,
You are then united
By the laws of your land.

It is a serious agreement
Which you enter into by choice,
But by your commitment
You make known your voice.

A covenant is established
To be forever true,
So never taint the union,
For God is watching you.

Even though He is not visible,
He sits high and looks low.
Your spouse may not be aware,
But He knows where ever you go.

Joining your body to another
Violates your spouse's trust;
So never betray your mate
Through unbridled lust.

The intimacy-seal must never be broken
To allow another in.
Adultery is no trivial matter,
Because God calls it sin.

When you sin against your mate,
Also, to God you're not true,
For when you made the pledge
You made an oath to him too.

If you, for any reason,
Don't protect your heart,
You'll fall in a weak moment
And not uphold your part.

If you go outside your marriage,
You'll begin to sink low,
And your sin will haunt you
Wherever you may go.

Though by grace you may recover,
There's no guarantee that you will,
So the safest thing for both
Is never to another yield.

What's Behind Flirting?

Flirting is not harmless,
Whatever one might think.
For it could cause destruction
Through a simple wink.

The giver may mean nothing by flirting,
And only considers it fun
But yet realize later
The harm that it has done.

Flirting could be something as simple
As an intentional stoop or bend,
But meant for the opposite sex,
To stir up lust within.

It could be an insinuation
That's hidden within a comment
But enough was implied by it,
To uncover its subtle intent.

It could be an intentional brush
Or a touch of hands or feet;
It could be an unholy glance
That undresses someone you meet.

Flirting is a conscious prelude
For adultery to take place.
If given the opportunity,
It'll find the time and space.

This is a character flaw
Which will cause one disgrace,
And it is displeasing to God
Whenever it takes place.

Viola T. Miller

It cannot be overlooked
Or in any way ignored,
For it is too costly
For a marriage to afford.

Adultery Is Folly

Like a bird flying from his nest
Is one's betrayal of love;
For it causes a downward spiral
From lack of connection above.

The unfaithful behaves irrationally,
As one with no sense,
For he/she is being enslaved
Without protection or defense.

Reasoning walks out the door
When confusion deceives the heart,
Then lies take up residence
And truth begins to depart.

Satan rejoices immensely
For the evil he has done,
Realizing he has marred
Beauty that was begun.

As insanity sets in temporarily,
"Up" then becomes "down."
Reality takes wings and flies,
And common sense cannot be found.

A stolen moment seems sweet at first,
But into bitterness it turns
When secrecy is uncovered,
And the truth everybody learns.

There is only one way out,
And God holds the key.
He'll unlock the prison,
If one desires to be free.

Confession must sincerely come
As forgiveness makes the call,
For only by full repentance
Is there restoration for all.

Viola T. Miller

Cast Down Imaginations

Wrong thoughts are inevitable,
But they're not a sin.
They come through open doors
And by meditation within.

When evil thoughts come,
They must be cast down,
For they won't remain inactive,
If allowed to hang around.

Temptation can only take over
When lust has been fed.
If it's not denied,
By the flesh one will be led.

If thoughts go unchecked
Imaginations will ensue,
Then Satan will find a way
To bind or entrap you.

Comparison opens a door.
Therefore, it's not wise;
Be assured it's usually sent
By your enemy in disguise.

It breeds thoughts of adultery
Which will draw your mind away,
Then imaginations will seize you
With torment every day.

The enemy appears as a friend
When seeking opportunity or
 space,
While subtly progressing
To an encounter face to face.

He'll deceive by some method
And insist that it's not wrong,
Convincing in some lying way
That you've missed out too long.

As a sheep walks willingly
Down his death trail,
By allowing lustful thoughts
All are bound to fail.

It'll seem harmless initially,
An excitement long overdue,
Just rest assured its calculation
Was designed to conquer you.

So recover yourself quickly,
And remember your spiritual life,
Don't become another statistic
Of a foolish husband or wife.

The Building Blocks to a Strong Marriage

Jealousy Can Be Acceptable

When is jealousy warranted,
And is considered right?
When does God condone it,
As acceptable in His sight?

There is a good jealousy,
One He doesn't mind;
It's the same He has
When loyalty He can't find.

God Himself is jealous
When his children go astray,
When with idols they're intimate
And walk in evil's way.

Being made in His image,
The same is part of man.
When infidelity causes jealousy,
It is easy to understand.

Marital love is to be exclusive
With each spouse the only other.
There's a breach in the union,
When love is shared with another.

Breaking this sacred trust
Is the worse betrayal of care.
It is the heaviest cross
A spouse could ever bear.

When one has forsaken all others
And pledged a spouse his/her life,
The cruelest of all fates
Is a cheating husband or wife.

Viola T. Miller

It is the worst of all let-downs
And the ultimate of rejection
Because one has given all,
Expecting mutual protection.

Overcoming Temptation

When temptations confront you,
Just think of the consequences,
Look unto God for help,
And He will supply defenses.

You must lift your mind
And gather your thoughts back;
Whatever is sent to tempt you
Is only Satan's attack.

So, reject temptation to evil
And don't receive the thought;
Command your own mind back
To think as you've been taught.

Nothing is worth infidelity,
So don't be led astray;
Choose to keep your covenant
To walk in an upright way.

Do not forsake your vows
And neither what you believe;
Through this evil suggestion,
Satan is trying to deceive.

Temptations only have power,
When they're yielded to,
And can only have authority
By something you say or do.

Be strong in your resistance,
For no temptation is too great.
You can escape its grasp,
And exit before it's too late.

Viola T. Miller

They have no substance
And that you well know,
So refuse to be fooled
By an unrealistic show.

The Building Blocks to a Strong Marriage

Working Through a Fall

In every confrontation
There's always grace for you,
No matter how difficult,
It can be conquered too.

It was by deception
You were knocked off your feet;
And it was not a situation
That you expected to meet.

Always keep in mind
God won't leave you alone
To face sinister plots
That are not your own.

For every problem one faces,
There's always help within.
Deliverance is available
Though you fall into sin.

You can depend on God;
His help is always there.
And He will gladly rescue
All who call in prayer.

So start with humility;
And in faith make your request.
Then receive your deliverance
And freedom from your test.

If one happens to fall
In a dark weak hour,
He/she can be restored
By God's forgiving power.

Understand it may take time
But be prepared to wait;
The fruit you expect to receive
Won't be a moment too late.

You may have been shaken,
But try putting it in the past;
By faith it's blotted out
And its memory will not last.

Though it seems impossible
And you're tempted by doubt,
Believe by faith in God,
And He will bring you out.

Viola T. Miller

Unfaithfulness Revealed

If your spouse has been unfaithful,
You must face the facts.
The betrayal is before you
As your mind continually attacks.

Your esteem is eroded
And your peace is shaken.
It's difficult to concentrate
And not feel forsaken.

The intrusion was a violation
When your mate became involved.
Ignoring it in pretense,
Won't get the problem solved.

If the one who's at fault
Tries to trivialize the deed,
Don't let it go unchallenged
And think you must concede.

In order to consider forgiveness,
Honesty must be employed.
If denial and lying remain,
All trust will be destroyed.

Adultery is no light affair
Regardless to society's view.
It should be considered
As disrespect for you.

Insistence on an accounting
Should not be a negotiable stand
But should be willingly offered
Without having any demand.

A complete and immediate break
Must be something that's evident.
A slow breaking away
Shouldn't be given your consent.

The one who is at fault
Is in no position to demand,
But should willingly submit
To cooperate all he/she can.

Viola T. Miller

Coping with Unfaithfulness

If you've been unfaithful
And violated your vow,
It is not impossible
To be redeemed somehow.

It all started from thoughts
And with them you can overcome.
First see yourself back
To where you fell from.

Don't try to make excuses,
But face up to your wrong.
No one made you fall,
You chose it on your own.

It is a serious matter,
Hard for any to repair,
But all things are possible
Through the Lord in prayer.

There is no easy solution
But pray and hope for the best.
Nothing is too hard for God
Whatever might be the test.

With all things considered
You're at the mercy of your mate,
For it's up to his/ her willingness
That will determine your fate.

Pray for another chance
And let it be understood,
Your promise of recommitment
Will indeed be made good.

If you are the victim
And not the one who did wrong,
The betrayal is so devastating
You may feel you can't go on.

First give yourself time;
You need to think things through.
Don't move too quickly
For at first, you won't know what
  to do.

After much thought and prayer,
You're better prepared for a
  decision,
And you can see more clearly
What should be your vision.

But you can work through
If it is your choice;
It'll be a long process,
Determined by what you voice.

Boundaries must be strictly set,
Not to ever be crossed,
Trust must be rebuilt again,
Or the relationship will be lost.

Working with God together
Forgiveness can be realized,
And all can be restored again
From what's been compromised.

Part Seven

Establishing a Strong Marriage

For the husband is the head of the wife as Christ is the head of the church...
Husbands love your wives, just as Christ loved the church and gave Himself up for her. (Ephesians 5:23a, 25, NIV)

Wives, submit to your husbands, as is fitting in the Lord.
Husbands love your wives and do not be harsh with them. (Colossians 3:18, 19)

By wisdom a house is built, and through understanding it is established; through knowledge its rooms are filled with rare and beautiful treasures.
The wise woman builds her house... (Proverbs 24:3; 14:1a, NIV)

Viola T. Miller

Marriage Can Be Wonderful

The marriage that remains
And weathers all storms,
Is not one that's man-made,
But one that God forms.

It doesn't matter how beautiful
A ceremony might be,
Only by God's planting
Can the lives become a tree.

His Word is the seed
Causing all things to grow,
And it is the fuel
Causing life's engines to go.

God must be acknowledged
And be honored as the head
And never be replaced
By something the world has said.

By Him there'll be joy
With the greatest impact;
By Him there's greatest fulfillment
And no invasion by lack.

It has all been written
In His timeless Book,
For all who'll treasure it,
And into it will look.

It shows the infinite benefit
For a man to cleave to his wife,
As both submit to each other
To experience sublime life.

All is defined clearly there,
Which gives life its worth
And causes a relationship
To mirror heaven on earth.

The Building Blocks to a Strong Marriage

Commitment Is Paramount

Commitment in a marriage
Pledges faithfulness to one,
Always remaining devoted
In all that's said or done.

It is first to God
That you promise you'll be true,
And that you'll be loyal
In whatever confronts you.

Then the way is paved
To always stay on track,
And remain determined
That you will not turn back.

To always be faithful
Will require one's all
When resisting intrusions
From an outsider's call.

It is by true commitment
That relationships are sealed,
And by it contrary notions
Will not be fulfilled.

Commitment locks in attention,
And it keeps others out.
It's what secures devotion
As it chases out doubt.

It cements love in place
And emits constant care.
Whether far or near
Trust is always there.

Some other may seem alluring
Or perhaps more appealing,
But commitment provides the stamina
To refrain from any yielding.

It will sustain the relationship
If all seems to be lost,
And will cause both to continue
Whatever might be the cost.

Without a firm commitment
Very little is nailed down,
For by its nature alone
Is true fidelity found.

Viola T. Miller

Get to Know Your Mate

Intimacy is not automatic.
For it, a price must be paid;
But it is attainable
When sincere efforts are made.

The way to know each other,
In almost all cases,
Is spending time together
On personal, close-knit basis.

By giving him/her priority
From determination to know,
True revelation will come forth
Because you won't let go.

Through relinquishing selfishness
And by keen observation,
Much can be learned of mates
By means of conversation.

When one speaks on issues,
There are unconscious revelations.
Insight can be gained by them
For views in other situations.

Not receiving constant gifts,
May get one partner down,
While another one's greater preference
Is having his/her mate around.

One might consider it love
When there's security from provisions,
While another receives the same
When trusted to make decisions.

Getting to know what one likes
And consciously locking it in
Is a sure point of indication
Which causes both to win.

Viola T. Miller

Prayer Is Essential

Prayer is reverencing One
Though He's out of sight,
The one who made us
And offers us His light.

It is our personal means
Of obtaining what we need,
And it is receiving a harvest
After planting a seed.

It is communion with God
In our Savior's name,
And waiting patiently in faith
As He processes our claim.

Prayer is the super helper
That keeps all in line;
And brings about a unity
One can't otherwise find.

Because it is impossible
To be at odds and be heard,
Prayer promotes peace
According to God's Word.

It inspires granting forgiveness
Before the time of prayer,
In order to be well assured
The Lord will meet you there.

When one insists on stubbornness,
Refusing to give or bend,
Prayer unclogs the heart
And ushers reason in.

When one is angry
With emotions out of control,
Prayer is the equalizer
Which restores back the mold.

Whenever trouble arises
And neither knows what to do,
Coming in prayer agreement
Will comfort and direct you.

When there are accusations
And both claim to be right,
Prayer will defuse tensions
And bring truth to light.

So prayer is a must-have
In all couples' lives,
In order for them to develop
Into mature husbands and wives.

Wisdom Is the Key

Only by His wisdom
Can any house stand
Because God drew the blueprint,
And He knows the plan.

Wisdom is too high
For one who is a fool
Because he refuses instruction
And plays by his own rule.

He's been everywhere
And knows it all,
No matter who summons him
He won't heed the call.

God's treasure of Wisdom
Can be opened by all,
If in simple humility
Any dares to call.

Wisdom imparts the cement
That holds all in place;
And the map needed
To direct the right way.

Wisdom is the peacemaker
When quarrels are started;
It is the enthusiasm
When relationships are half-hearted.

Wisdom is our truth
When we're tempted to lie;
It is our cause to continue
When there's no reason why.

Viola T. Miller

So submitting to God's wisdom
From a decision within
Is the surest guarantee
That a marriage will not end.

The Building Blocks to a Strong Marriage

Crucial Principles

One crucial principle
Is to learn to disagree
Because no married couple
From this will be free.

But to know how to manage
And express your view,
Will require humility
And determination from you.

If one of you is angry,
Let the other remain sane.
Resist temptation to shout
Or to yell out blame.

Be alert to the danger
Of waiting too long,
Before either one addresses
Something both know is wrong.

It is a mistaken idea
That it will soon go away;
For it only goes underground
To be revived some day.

Don't silence dissatisfaction
By giving it a place inside;
It'll not remain there
Nor will it continue to hide.

Make it your policy
To greet one another each day.
Never allow another's opinion
To obstruct your way.

Make it a rule together
That as one, you must pray,
And be sure to do it
At least once a day.

Always be quick to forgive
And quick to let go;
Because when no seeds are sown,
Then no plants can grow.

Be quick to say "I'm sorry,"
And I've made a mistake;
Be quick to grant the mercy,
Of which you partake.

Be quick to notice good,
And faults try not to find,
Hardly notice what's negative,
And quickly put it out of mind.

Always be quick to listen,
And slowly demand your view;
Be quick to credit your spouse
And let him/her exalt you.

Be quick to humble yourself
For God resists the proud;
Remember truth isn't validated
Just because it's loud.

Be quick to understand failure,
By considering your last fall;
Be quick to refuse judgments
When they upon you call.

Be quick to volunteer help
And of all your own share,
Then when you have lack
Help for you will be there.

Viola T. Miller

Protecting the Relationship

Most don't mind correction
When they are all alone
As long as it's not public,
But privately done at home.

When done around others,
It embarrasses and causes shame;
Though it may be passed off
As though it were a game.

When one publicly boasts
And shows off what he/she knows,
The other partner feels inferior
From the conceit that shows.

That drives a couple apart,
Possibly without intent;
Because it shows no respect
By the messages that are sent.

When one declares freedom
And independence on his/ her own,
That portrayal as an individual,
Causes disconnection in the home.

A relationship only flourishes
When each functions as a part,
Supplying what is needed
To promote singleness of heart.

When one doesn't feel honored,
But instead feels put down,
Soon thoughts will come to mind
Of not being wanted around.

The Building Blocks to a Strong Marriage

If this is not the intent,
Let the message then be clear,
So that restoration and wholeness
Will wash away all fear.

Viola T. Miller

Financial Security

With financial misunderstandings
Always come division,
Giving confusion a place,
When making a decision.

If either one is selfish,
Only thinking of him/herself,
There'll surely be contentions,
And there'll be no funds left.

Neither should purchase items
The income can't cover,
And then secretly hide them
To deceive each other.

When one is a waster
And will carelessly spend,
There'll be little for savings
On which to depend.

Both spouses should be included
When major spending is done,
And impulsive purchasing
Shouldn't be done by either one.

When one doesn't agree,
The other shouldn't go ahead,
And continue right on spending
No matter what's said.

Care should be taken
To formulate a plan,
To keep up with spending
And work hand in hand.

There should be preparation
For emergencies that arise
Because life has a way
Of greeting us with surprise.

Savings don't just happen
And discipline is hard to enforce,
But the lack of it in crisis
May contribute to divorce.

A couple's financial security
Should be a definite goal.
The ignoring of it
May cause a marriage to fold.

The Building Blocks to a Strong Marriage

Keep Romance Alive

Romance doesn't just happen
And neither will it stay,
If it is not nourished
And fed every day.

Pursue it with passion
And give it no rest.
Let it not grow weak
But keep it at its best.

Do not let it slip,
But keep romance alive.
It is mortar for the bricks
That helps a marriage survive.

If you are not determined
It will surely die;
Soon you will grow apart,
And then you'll wonder why.

To notice the insignificant
Is a powerful seed to sow;
For it produces a harvest
That keeps romance aglow.

It is worth all the effort
Required of you to do.
To keep the oils of joy
Continually flowing for you.

Sweet words keep it alive
And thoughtful loving deeds.
So without hesitation,
Seek to meet each other's needs.

Do it by laying aside
What your plans demand,
And continuously deferring,
In every way you can.

It should be innovative
And something from your heart,
Something you keep doing
Just as from the start.

Present unexpected gifts,
And write personal notes or cards,
Call just to say, "I love you"
And warm each other's hearts.

Make every effort you can
To find reasons to touch,
Though you're aware of your love
Keep telling each other how much.

For romance activation,
Sex need not be the goal,
But by continual closeness
Stimulation can easily unfold.

Romance will unconsciously slip
As you gradually follow routines,
And you cease to verbalize
How much each other means.

You'll know that it has slipped
Or it's in the process,
When you never plan
Just for happiness.

Viola T. Miller

The Need for Nurturing

Before the marriage takes place,
Nurturing is easily done.
This is mainly true
Since attention is only on one.

But as time moves along,
And responsibilities increase,
It is all too easy
For nurturing to cease.

As other demands are answered,
And there're different problems to face,
Nurturing will often get forced
Somewhere out of place.

If it is left ignored,
It won't go away;
Trouble just silently brews
And soon will have its day.

Smart spouses have understanding
And work at being aware,
Supplying needed affirmation
Which communicates their care.

When it comes to wives needs
Few husbands have a clue,
So wives for the most part,
Must inform them what to do.

If one needs something more
And is not satisfied,
Let the other listen
And see that it is not denied.

The Building Blocks to a Strong Marriage

>A willingness to sow
>Will cause reaping time too,
>And the harvest will be plentiful
>To be enjoyed by you.

Viola T. Miller

Take Time for Each Other

Take time for each other
Even if something has to go.
It may not seem feasible,
But afterwards you'll know.

It's easy to fall into a rut,
And it won't happen over night,
But it will come on gradually
Unless you have wisdom and insight.

Come aside for special times
And don't let them be neglected,
Make time to take the time,
So you will stay protected.

It may not be expensive,
But it must be exclusive;
See that all others are forsaken
And only you two are inclusive.

Let there be appreciation occasions
Which one or the other plans,
When the two of you sit and talk
And perhaps stroke or hold hands.

This may be a called time,
When one feels the need.
It really matters not
Which one chooses to lead.

If it is regularly scheduled
And is done by date,
Whenever it is desirable,
There is no need to wait.

The benefits will be super
And well worth the while.
This should be a "must"
Whatever is your lifestyle.

Viola T. Miller

Identifying Needs

What one perceives as a need
May be trivial to his/her spouse.
It's because of the upbringings
Which were different in each
 house.

One may think of closeness
As something that's automatic,
But if it is ignored,
To the other, it may be traumatic.

The reason for the difference
May be perceived or real.
In any case it's there,
And must be addressed still.

One may not be affected
By no hugs and kissing,
While the other spouse is
 devastated
Because these are missing.

Though it may not be spoken,
Both know something is there.
It is like a big monster
That won't go any where.

If one suffers in silence
While the other is unaware,

It can't be corrected
Unless it's known to be there.

It won't just disappear,
Or simply go away,
But will only worsen
If it's allowed to stay.

Attempts at other endeavors
Will hit a brick wall,
And everything will fail
For no one answers the call.

This'll bring on a war,
Which to one makes sense,
But the very same thing,
Places the other on defense.

The maze seems endless,
With no peaceable solution,
But by prayer and counsel
There can be resolution.

The one with the need
Must convey it to his/her mate.
It should be given priority
And not allowed to wait.

The Building Blocks to a Strong Marriage

Sex and Spirituality

Sex was God's idea,
And all He made was good.
When in its proper place,
It'll be all that it should.

By it, a new being is conceived
And then comes a new life.
This was God's choice
Through a husband and his wife.

God's first husband and wife
Were naked and not ashamed;
They enjoyed pure love and freedom
When sin wasn't yet named.

Restrictions were put in place
To keep out intrusion,
But one's mate wasn't intended
As part of that exclusion.

Old wives tales and myths
Have been passed down and taught.
They've caused many women
To shun sexual thought.

Satan plays on ignorance
Which gives him a place to hide.
Then he can accuse the innocent
Who wrestle with desires inside.

One needs not be ignorant
Unless there's refusal to learn.

Spirituality is not promoted
By no sexual concern.

When a wife receive nothing from sex
Other than satisfying her man,
It won't be very long
That she'll avoid it if she can.

The understanding of sexuality
And the sanctity of it all,
Has locked many relationships
And caused marriages to fall.

All the areas in question
Should have answers made clear,
Then the time of consummation
Wouldn't be met with fear.

Making love shouldn't be a tolerance,
Or for one partner's benefit.
But it should be mutually satisfying
With joyful excitement for it.

Since the time of puberty
Or perhaps before,
Sexual arousal and fulfillment
Were locked behind a door.

God sanctions it in marriage
With freedom to meet that need.
It's to be welcomed by both,
In thought, word and deed.

Viola T. Miller

Is My Marriage Divorce Proof?

What causes divorce?
Who can really tell?
What really goes wrong,
That causes a marriage to fail?

Does one desire something
The other refuses to give?
Or, are divorces unavoidable
In the society in which we live?

How is my foundation?
Was it laid right?
Was our courtship long-term?
Or did it blossom overnight?

What about our convictions?
Do we know where we stand?
On important issues,
Do we walk hand in hand?

How is the financial harmony
Within our household?
Are there secret contentions,
Either one should unfold?

Is there joy with each other,
Or just tolerance at best?
Is my spouse pleasing to me?
Or does he/she flunk the test?

Are we at ease together?
Or uncomfortable being alone?
Do we search for excuses to leave
Because the spark is gone?

How much of my attention
Do I give to my spouse?
Are most of my interests
Found outside of my house?

Do I find that it is easy
Showing others that I care,
Yet when it comes to my spouse,
I find I'm lacking there?

Are we close friends
In truth without a doubt?
Do we flow freely together,
And enjoy just hanging out?

Do we support each other
And seldom find fault,
Maintaining connection in absence
By deliberate thought?

Do I fear that someday,
My spouse may have an affair
Or that I may wake up one day
And he/she won't be there?

Do we have open communication
With freedom of expression?
Are we transparent with each other,
Not given to false impression?

Are we helpers to each other,
Always standing side by side?

The Building Blocks to a Strong Marriage

Sensitive and clothed with
  humility,
Not allowing pride to abide?

Is Christ the head of our lives?
Do we trust in Him alone?
Is he the first one consulted
Whenever things go wrong?

Do I respect my spouse,
Including him/her in my plans?
Before I make decisions,
Do I see where he/she stands?

When it comes to needs,
Are mine being met?
Do I have expectations
I've not experienced yet?

Do I often struggle,
Pursuing my rightful place?

Do I feel I'm cheated
And granted very little space?

Do we spend time together,
Or do we seldom speak?
Are we drawing closer
Or is the relationship weak?

Do we ever pray together,
Asking blessings for each other?
Or is it a strain to share
And face one another?

Honest answers will indicate
What we can plainly see,
And if we've strayed away
From where we should be.

Is my marriage strong
In its present state?
Should adjustments be made
To redirect its fate?

Viola T. Miller

Watch Your Words

By words we empower each other,
And by them, our lives we direct.
It's by the words we speak,
We guard, deliver and protect.

It's by what's spoken forth
That we experience good or bad;
And by what we utter,
We're made happy or sad.

By the words that we speak,
Our spouses, we can make
And by our choice of words,
Their spirits, we can break.

With words we cause comfort,
Or through them, come pain;
Therefore, from evil,
May our lips refrain.

Words can minister peace,
And they can enforce health.
Poverty can ride upon them,
Or they can promote wealth.

They can cause condemnation,
Or set captives free;
They can uncover the hidden
That truth, all may see.

Words can minister confidence,
Or they can cause fear;
The effect of one word
Can destroy everything dear.

From the words that we speak,
We have what we say;
So speaking what we desire
Is what directs our way.

Since words are so important
And can powerfully affect a life,
Speaking the right words is crucial
To every husband and wife.

Viola T. Miller

Understanding Submission

When two are competing,
And desiring the leading role,
There's a power struggle
For who will be in control.

God ordained the husband
To be the head of his wife,
As they share together
In their married life.

Submission in many areas
Applies to husband and wife,
As they respect each other
While building a prosperous life.

How is this implemented,
When by each it's considered?
It must be understood
That no one be embittered.

Submission is considering your
  mate
And seeking to understand.
It's working with each other
As cooperatively as you can.

It's checking with each other
Before major decisions are made;
It's receiving spousal approval
Before seeking another's aid.

It is not being stubborn
And going on ahead,
When both cannot agree
On something that's been said.

It is seeking cooperatively,
In peace to abide,
And not doing deliberately
What is known to divide.

It's maintaining your composure
Though your project was
  rejected;
And not taking it personally
As long as you're respected.

It's not seeking revenge
And making your partner pay,
For something you've wanted
But didn't get your way.

It's respecting your mate's wishes;
And though you don't agree,
There's no flaunting of freedom
For every one to see.

It's having a willingness
To find a compromise.
It's not being selfish
But for fairness in both eyes.

It is gently confronting
What you know is not right,
And refusing peacefully
What's wrong in God's sight.

The Building Blocks to a Strong Marriage

It's allowing your spouse to go on
Though you know he/she's
　wrong;
It is speaking out calmly
As to what you won't condone.

It is seeking God's help
And trusting in His grace.
Through His wisdom and insight,
Unity will take place.

Viola T. Miller

Confronting Problems

Confrontation cannot be avoided
When there's something wrong;
Pushing it down or back
Can't last for very long.

So come together and talk,
And let nothing block your way.
With God's help and guidance
You'll know what to say.

Before anything takes place,
Emotions should be controlled,
Then the issue at hand
Will be easy to unfold.

A time should be set
Which both can agree to.
Let nothing be a hindrance
To prevent your working through.

Determine to be courteous
And hear each other out;
Ask necessary questions politely
If understanding is in doubt.

Whatever is on your mind,
Let your spouse know.
It's important what you say
And the attitude that you show.

Was it something done,
Or something that was said?
What brought on the spirit
By which you're being led?

Whatever has been done,
It won't go away,
Unless it's addressed squarely,
Then it cannot stay.

Your lives have flowed together
With the peacefulness of rivers.
The harmony you've enjoyed,
Only God Himself delivers.

You've conquered all other storms,
Whether in rocky or calm weather;
So this one is no different,
If you'll work it out together.

So make every effort,
To give Satan no space.
Remember He has no power
Unless he's given a place.

It could come through a word,
Or be allowed by a thought;
It could come through imaginations,
Which only come to naught.

Whatever the problem is,
It's lasted far too long.
So let it reign no longer
And return to being strong.

Part Eight

The Power of Love

Love is very patient and kind, never jealous or envious, never boastful or proud, never haughty, or selfish or rude. Love does not demand its own way. It is not irritable or touchy. It does not hold grudges and will hardly even notice when others do it wrong.

If you love someone, you will be loyal to him no matter what the cost. You will always believe in him, always expect the best of him, and always stand your ground in defending him. (I Corinthians 13:4, 5, 7, TLB)

Most important of all, continue to show deep love for each other, for love covers a multitude of sins. (I Peter 4:8, NLT)

Viola T. Miller

Love's Character

Love is the greatest connector,
More than meets the eye,
It can prevail continually
And needs no reason why.

Word expressions for love
May be hard to find,
But the power in its glue
Binds the recipient in mind.

It embraces openness
And willingly ventures risk.
It's not easily discouraged
But it will constantly persist.

Love refrains from dominating
And respects your spouse's views.
When assistance is needed
It will not refuse.

Love is ever so sensitive
To any need discovered,
And it willingly accommodates
To see that it is covered.

It examines cause and effect
And takes note of each reaction.
It carefully avoids negativity
In order to cause no faction.

Love is never selfish,
But will share its all.
It will be ever present
And doesn't need a call.

It will not draw attention
But will remain out of sight;
Only by its deeds
Does it ever come to light.

It will overlook wrong
Instead of pointing it out.
It'll holdfast to confidence
When there is reason to doubt.

Love holds to only good
And forgives whatever is bad;
It seeks to bring joy
When ever the loved is sad.

Love really conquers all
And will cause all to be well.
The power of its might
Causes marriages not to fail.

The Humility of Love

Love is always humble
And it's never proud;
It is never puffed up,
Nor contentiously loud.

Love refuses any engagement
In a struggle for power;
For it knows the consequences
Will make a relationship sour.

When mates shut down
And refuse to hear,
Both will suffer the loss
From not yielding the ear.

Both stand to benefit
And much could be gained,
If pride were dethroned
And humility were retained.

The humility of love
Will take a low place,
For it's not threatened
By what it might face.

Difference doesn't mean wrong
Neither does it mean inferior,
Nor does it give an edge
For one to feel superior.

Refusing to humble one's self
Will only build a wall,
And this is often responsible
For causing a marriage to fall.

But all can be turned around
When humility is given a place,
And both ask for help
To solve whatever they face.

Humility promotes respect
And frees from nagging stress.
It communicates worth
And lays fear to rest.

As humility is displayed
The same will be extended,
And the effect will be obvious
When all's forgiven and mended.

So open up your heart
And unstop your ears;
Learn from each other
And rid yourselves of fears.

Because of its humility,
Love will long endure;
Trusting that in all things
God's word remains sure.

Viola T. Miller

How a Spouse Communicates Love

Love is communicated
Through words that endear,
And the reality of it
Comes by being near.

Whether it's in thought,
In word or in deed,
Love produces a harvest
That will fulfill every need.

It is communicated
In the tone one speaks,
And glory for itself,
It never seeks.

Love is communicated
By seeking to understand,
As it endeavors to be cooperative
In all the ways it can.

Love is communicated
By simple embraces,
And by looking intently
Into each other's faces.

It is communicated
By patience in action,
When constant care is taken
That insures satisfaction.

Love is communicated
When gratitude is evident,
When one strives to remember
Every special occasion or event.

Love is communicated
By listening to the one you love,
And interacting willingly
With whatever is spoken of.

It is communicated
By willingness to negotiate,
And by promptly noticing
What it should appreciate.

Love is communicated
By always being a friend,
By always being faithful
And loyal till the end.

It is communicated
By speaking what is true,
And refusing to condone
What it knows will hurt you.

Finally, it's communicated
When at nothing it will stop,
But continually perseveres
Till its loved one is on top.

The Building Blocks to a Strong Marriage

Love's Behavior

Love never relaxes
When there're things to be done,
And there's no one to help
Except the loved one.

Love won't sit idly,
Leaving everything to a mate,
And not lift a finger
To lighten the weight.

If love is only in word
But is without action,
It will appear superficial
And will soon cause faction.

It has no substance
When it's only verbalized,
And it leaves itself open
That it be criticized.

True love is genuine
In word and in deed,
And it will give its all
That its object has no need.

Love will be disciplined
And pick up behind itself,
Quickly replacing everything
Right back on its shelf.

It will give itself feet,
And rise to meet the occasion,
Having no need for prompting
And no need for persuasion.

Love won't make assertions
Declaring it understands,
While it continues right on
Making unreasonable demands.

Love will be considerate
And will not overly require,
But will praise what's done
As it takes time to admire.

Love notices achievements
And quickly gives commendation,
Always ready to encourage
In every situation.

It won't take for granted
As if it has a slave,
But because it's appreciative,
It knows how to behave.

Love makes itself alert
And seeks to find a way,
To contribute to its loved one
Having a special day.

It will recognize the moment
And swing with the slightest sign,
Being ready momentarily
To create a special time.

Deferring to its object,
Love makes itself known,
By displaying its characteristics,
Which are abundantly shown.

Viola T. Miller

Many have misconceptions
When it comes to love,
But its true definition
Comes from God up above.

He, being the essence of it,
Put it on open display,
When He gave His all
On Calvary one day.

The Building Blocks to a Strong Marriage

Tough Love

Sometimes love is tough
In order to correct,
Though it not be accepted,
Yet it's needed to protect.

Love must not draw back
To obtain an acceptable place,
For if needed correction is lacking
More serious problems it'll face.

By moving ahead anyway
Though it's not received,
Love will produce fruit
That saves from being deceived.

Love refuses to flatter
Though it may be sought,
But truth is more lasting
When it's lovingly taught.

Tough love may cause separation
Because it's not desired,
But its fruit is much better
Than empty words admired.

Tough love speaks against wrong,
When it becomes aware.
Even when it's rejected
Counsel will still be there.

It is stronger than heartache,
And it's deeper than
  misunderstanding.
It's greater than harsh words
And more effective than
  demanding.

Being more than a thought or
  feeling,
Love is really a choice;
Yet it has untold benefits
Through its peaceful voice.

It's more than emotions
For they come and go,
But true love is steadfast
Though impulses may not know.

It will continue to stand,
Come what will or may,
And it can always be trusted
To walk in wisdom's way.

Viola T. Miller

Love's Forbidden List

Don't bring up dead issues
To give yourself an edge,
You'll never win with them
But drive a deeper wedge.

Never highlight weaknesses,
Whatever your mate may do,
For that's hard to overcome
And will condemn you.

Never attack your mate,
Hoping to get revenge.
It won't serve its purpose
And neither one will win.

Never seek to outshine your
  partner,
By putting him/her down,
Or by speaking disparagingly
When others are around.

Never discuss with your children
Problems concerning your spouse.
It only serves negatively
To promote a divided house.

Don't ever overspend,
Hoping to pay your spouse back.
Somehow in the run of things,
You will experience the lack.

Don't behave in a childish manner
By talking to your mate through
  another;
If you can't talk directly,
Don't imply it through some
  other.

Don't allow comparisons,
For they generally will divide,
And whatever causes division
Won't continue to hide.

Negatives cause contentions
Which will surely cause a rift,
Then it's almost impossible
For them to ever lift.

Don't bring up ancestry
When the moment is heated;
All attempts to take it back
Will only be defeated.

Never open old wounds
Which you've worked to heal;
All old settled issues
Must remain under seal.

Don't allow your pride
To keep an exalted place,
For in a very short while
The truth you must face.

Don't work against your partner
In order to get ahead,
And don't side with another
On something you two have said.

The Building Blocks to a Strong Marriage

Don't withhold attention,
Hoping to find out what's missing;
It's not by levying punishment
That your partner agrees to listen.

Seek to be a blessing
And work to enhance love;
Then whatever is missing,
God supplies from above.

Part Nine

Examine Yourself as a Spouse

The Lord is watching everywhere, keeping His eye on both the evil and the good. (Proverbs 15:3, NLT)

Don't criticize, and then you won't be criticized. (Matthew 7:1, TLB)

Only by pride cometh contentions: but with the well advised is wisdom. (Proverbs 13:10, KJV)

Let no corrupt communication proceed out of your mouth, but that which is good to the use of edifying… (Ephesians 4:29, KJV)

A nagging wife is as annoying as the constant dripping on a rainy day. Trying to stop her complaints is like trying to stop the wind or hold something with greased hands. (Proverbs 27:15, NLT).

Can two walk together, except they be agreed? (Amos 3:3, KJV)

The Building Blocks to a Strong Marriage

What Kind of Mate Are You?

Are you the kind of mate
Who is one of a kind?
The one who epitomizes
What your spouse had in mind?

Are you the kind of mate
Who's indifferent toward your spouse,
While you busy yourself
With chores around the house?

Are you a spouse in ministry
Who is seldom at home,
And often your family
Must make it on its own?

Are you that mate
Who glues to televisions,
And won't take the time
To make important decisions?

Are you one of those
Who appear to be laid back,
But when it comes to others
You seem to suffer no lack?

Are you a spouse who ministers
And have patience with everyone?
Yet when it comes to your mate,
It seems that you have none?

Are you that kind of spouse
With no interest in your mate,
Yet time spent with others
Is as though it were a date?

For them, nothing's too much
And no time is too long;
They may ask anything
And nothing's considered wrong.

Are you the kind of spouse
Who frivolously spends,
And though you're in debt,
Your spending never ends?

What about that spouse
Who wants control of assets,
To keep your mate from spending,
So you can make debts?

Or, are you that spouse
Who is tight as a drum,
And you're very difficult
To get anything from?

Are you that spouse
Who to everyone else, is nice,
Yet to your own mate,
You are as cold as ice?

Or perchance are you one
Who pushes your mate away,
By using the empty words,
"Maybe another day?"

Viola T. Miller

If your answers were honest
And "yes" to most of these,
Then it must be obvious
Your mate, you don't please.

As you face yourself
And you see the light,
Only apologies and repentance
Can make everything right.

God is willing to forgive,
If you take the first step;
But if you are not,
This marriage, He can't help.

The Building Blocks to a Strong Marriage

Do I Communicate Well?

Most marriages break up
From communication being
　neglected;
Or, all of the attempts at it,
Have constantly been rejected.

Where could it begin?
Who would be to blame?
Who could be the first one
To snuff out the flame?

As I honestly check myself
I vow that I'll be true;
I'll abide by my findings
And do what I'm told to do:

Do I remain courteous,
And work at being calm,
Though I feel emotionally
There's cause for alarm.

Am I always respectful?
Do I endeavor to use tact?
When an issue has been settled,
Do I often bring it back?

Do I ever unconsciously
Cause my spouse pain,
Because at the moment
I think it brings me gain?

Am I ever insensitive,
And won't offer a helping hand?

Do I ever remain indifferent
And not seek to understand?

When I disapprove of something,
How is it brought to attention?
By careful consideration?
Or some provocative mention?

When an issue comes up,
Must I always be right?
If I don't win a discussion,
Does it erupt into a fight?

Do I ever raise my voice,
Attempting to dominate?
As a means of control,
Do I try to intimidate?

Do I take the answer, "no"
As a personal attack?
Do I revert to silence
As a mean of fighting back?

Do I always listen carefully,
And not think on ahead?
Do I pay close attention,
To understand what's said?

According to my answers
To almost all of these,
With our communication
Am I well pleased?

Viola T. Miller

Do I Nag?

Am I a quarrelsome wife,
Like a constant drip?
Have I continuous chatter
From a complaining lip?

Am I a treasure hunter,
Seeking what I can find?
Even when nothing is wrong
Do I continue to whine?

When all is well with me,
Am I satisfied?
Do I just rest contented,
Allowing peace to abide?

Do I continually remind
Though there is no need?
When it's brought to attention,
Do I stop indeed?

Am I so busy checking,
I forget how much I'm blessed?
What I require of my spouse
Can I pass the test?

Detecting a tiny speck
Is deception in disguise.
It conceals our own plank,
Which covers over our eyes.

The gracious thing to do
Is make allowances for all,
Considering our own selves
Lest we too should fall.

The Building Blocks to a Strong Marriage

> As I adjust my focus
> And myself honestly face,
> May I work on my faults
> As God gives me the grace.

Viola T. Miller

Am I Mean?

Am I a mean person,
One hard to entreat?
Am I mostly unpleasant,
To those whom I meet?

Am I hard to get along with,
Surly most of my days,
Negative in my thinking,
And unyielding in my ways.

Am I mostly judgmental,
And often harsh and rude?
Do I use tact in expressions,
Or, do they provoke a feud?

What vibes do I emit?
Do I really care?
Do I bear others crosses
Which they find hard to bear?

Are my words cutting
Because they're cruel or cold?
Am I in denial of myself,
And passing off myself as bold?

If I were on the other side
And a victim of a person like me,
Would I appear repulsive
And despise what I see?

Does my spouse seem honored
Because he/she has me around?
Or does it seem all too often
Few positives can be found?

Am I really ill-tempered
And quick to pick a fight?
Is it because to me,
Very little seems right?

As I submit to scrutiny
What does God reveal?
Am I what I could be,
If I'd yield to His will?

Do I want to change,
Because I hate what I see?
Am I willing to concede
The problem is really in me?

The undesirable traits
Can be removed inside.
But that will only take place
When faults, we cease to hide.

Though we can't change
  ourselves,
Still change is close by.
By calling to God for help,
He'll hear and answer our cry.

The changes that will take place
Are more than words can say,
But their fruitful evidence
Will display itself each day.

If I have passed his test,
I'm my spouse's crown.
He wears me so proudly
As joy in me is found.

Am I Proud?

Do I resent needed correction,
Though I know that I'm wrong?
Do I sacrifice what's right
That I stay on the throne?

Do I feel humiliation,
When my spouse I must ask,
Because for some requirement
I'm inadequate for a task?

How do I characterize myself?
Do I feel I'm superior?
Somewhere in my mind,
Do I consider my mate inferior?

Must I place myself first,
Or I'll do nothing at all?
Must I be above only,
Or I feel that I'm too small?

Do I resent praise for my mate,
And I want it to quickly fade?
Yet, it is greatly received,
When over me it's made?

Do I notice every detail,
Whenever it applies to me?
But the achievements of my mate
Somehow I can't see?

Do I find it hard to share,
When my mate has a need?
Do I bless him/her in word only,
Or from my heart indeed?

As I consider these questions,
And all answers in each case,
Should I conclude honestly
I have pride I must face?

Viola T. Miller

Am I Truthful?

God knows all about me,
All I say and do,
But what about my spouse?
Does he/she know me too?

Am I hiding any secrets
That I hope he/she will never
  know?
Am I holding to some things
Knowing I should let them go?

Do I exaggerate facts
To make the outcome great?
Do I pretend ignorance
To cover up my being late?

Do I accept another's credit
Right down to the letter,
And yet never confess it
Even though I know better?

Do I ever keep silent
When I know I should speak out?

Do I pretend I'm convinced
Though I'm full of doubt?

Can my spouse trust me?
Will I always do right?
Can I be trusted in all cases,
Though he/she's out of sight?

Do I imply or insinuate
By body language or acts,
By distorted truth or deceptions,
Or by some twisted facts?

Are there a few areas
Of which I should take care?
Must I admit to myself and God
Sometimes lies are there?

As I check my answers
And face what I've found,
Truth I must embrace,
And speak only what's sound.

The Building Blocks to a Strong Marriage

Am I Committed?

How serious is my marriage?
Is it to me a vow?
Am I giving my best,
To keep it strong somehow?

Am I determined in my heart,
To allow nothing within;
Nothing that will entice me
And cause me to sin?

Is my spouse dear to me,
Closer than any other?
Do I consider him/her first,
Before I do another?

Do I face all of our issues,
Determined to press through?
Do I ever entertain divorce,
As the best thing to do?

Do I stand with my spouse,
And to him/her truly cleave?
Do I work through circumstances,
Which say that I should leave?

Will I willingly seek help,
When I've tried my very best,
Yet nothing seems promising
That we can pass the test.

Would my loyalty transcend
Beyond what I feel?
If my emotions changed,
Could I continue on by my will still?

What if conditions changed
Beyond my spouse's control?
Would I leave him/her helpless
Because something disturbed my goal?

Would I let my marriage fold
Because of something unforeseen?
Even though it occurred,
Could my spouse upon me lean?

Could I just look to God
And continue on ahead,
Believing in my heart
That by faith I'd be led?

Am I truly determined,
"Until death do we part?"
Will I honor my vows forever,
As I promised from the start?

I believe I am committed
And my loyalty is in place.
Through God we'll conquer
Whatever conditions we face.

Part Ten

Conflict Resolutions

If a house is divided against itself, that house cannot stand. (Mark 3:25, NIV)

Get rid of all bitterness, rage, anger, harsh words, and slander, as well as all types of malicious behavior. Instead, be kind to each other, tenderhearted, forgiving one another, just as God through Christ has forgiven you. (Ephesians 4:31, 32, NLT)

But if you are bitterly jealous and there is selfish ambition in your heart don't brag about being wise. That is the worse kind of lie. For jealousy and selfishness are not God's kinds of wisdom. Such things are earthly, unspiritual, and motivated by the devil.
But the wisdom that comes from heaven ...peace loving, gentle at all times, and willing to yield to others. It is full of mercy and good deeds. (James 3:14, 15, 17, NLT)

Attitude for Resolutions

Examine your own heart
And give God the right of way;
Pledge that you'll abide by
Whatever He might say.

Remember that He is good
And will reveal perfect design,
Though it may not be at all
What you had in mind.

But openness to truth
Is pleasing in His sight,
And through His holy Word
He shines forth His light.

Often we have blind spots
And think others are at fault,
So we can't see readily
The lies we have bought.

Confession of known mistakes
Will quickly clear the air,
And make both hearts pliable
If resentment is found there.

Have anticipation of resolution
Because God knows it all,
And when all is in His hands
Every wall must fall.

Stand fast in pursuit of truth
Though there is an easier track.
If the issue isn't dealt with properly,
Before long, it will be back.

Viola T. Miller

All we need is available
If we'd only ask;
God has the solution
Whatever is the task.

Something's Wrong

One of the true revealers
That something isn't right,
Is creating longer hours
Away from home at night.

Another is making the children
The priority of your life
Because it's no more joy
In being a husband or a wife.

It may be feeling boredom
At the thought of your spouse,
Or just feeling better
With him/her out the house.

It may be throwing yourself
Wholeheartedly into your career
Because you feel uneasy
From something that you fear.

It may be replacing your spouse
With a hobby or a pet
Because of your frustration
Or being often upset.

The point of hindrance
Which you cannot get past,
Must be confronted soon
Or the marriage will not last.

By checking on your status
You may realize all the more,
Divorce is now knocking
Right outside your door.

Both may have realized
Something must be done,
But neither has come forward,
But waited for the other one.

Whatever the problem may be,
It can indeed be solved.
Whenever there's an impasse,
Always get God involved.

Viola T. Miller

Hidden Offenses

It could happen to you
And you may not know it;
You could have strife inside,
But you do not show it.

Though you don't attend to it,
You know something's wrong.
Yet you push it down inside
And keep moving right along.

Mentally, you think to yourself
It really doesn't count,
But inside you've become aware
That tension's beginning to
  mount.

Your emotions made a note
When you pushed it down.
They quickly brought it back,
When no one was around.

A feeling of unrest
Began to build a case,
And you weren't even aware
That something had taken place.

Some kind of unknown feeling
Began gnawing at your mind.
You tried to locate it,
But it, you couldn't find.

Then something similar happened
Which reminded you anew,
That which you kept inside
Had really offended you.

The issue was not addressed
Or uprooted from its space,
So freedom wasn't granted to you
And peace could claim no place.

It must be dealt with,
In order to have peace,
For if it isn't removed,
Disconnection will not cease.

Satan Is to Blame

No matter who is right
Things are not the same.
Only by coming together
Can truth remove the blame.

Come and reason together
And make your claims known.
Don't let some triviality
In you, become full blown.

Lay the problem and blame
Upon whom it is due;
The source of it all
Is not your mate or you.

The devil has managed to succeed
In concocting something untrue
And you've wasted precious time
With accusations not from you.

As a roaring lion,
He sought you to devour,
And because you weren't alert,
You were deceived somehow.

But the truth is out now,
And even though it loomed,
Thank God by grace and mercy,
You were not consumed.

Beginning now, make up your mind
If you want everything straight.
Initiate a kiss and make up;
There is no need to wait.

Viola T. Miller

Eating Your Words

When you've spoken harshly
And know that you were wrong,
Admit it right a way,
And don't let it be too long.

Your spouse has done nothing
So why the attack?
To find out the truth,
Just trace your steps back.

Something was on your mind
But you kept it hidden,
Refusing to discuss it
Though that was forbidden.

That was Satan's entry
Which caused you to fall.
You weren't spiritually alert
To the tempter's call.

Your words can't be recalled,
But you can apologize.
Humility is the pathway
Which leads to becoming wise.

"Sorry" is a very small word,
But it carries great weight;
And it is most effective
When it is not too late.

So, go in repentance
And erase the attack;
Do whatever is needed
To get yourself on track.

Admit you were the one off,
And you desire grace,
For through unchecked hostility,
Torment was given a place.

Admit you weren't alert,
And your focus was divided;
So when Satan slipped in,
You realized you had sided.

Admitting that you're wrong
Is not an easy task,
But it will be easier
If it's done without a mask.

As you go and eat your words
And seek yourself to redeem,
It won't be nearly as difficult
As Satan makes it seem.

The Building Blocks to a Strong Marriage

Resolving Conflicts

Most conflicts are best resolved
When there's a structural plan
Because there's not much thinking
When things are out of hand.

The plan should be constructed
By both partners involved;
And they should agree to
　diligently work
Until all problems are solved.

If the agreement that's made
Favors either of the two,
It will not work effectively,
And the plan will fall through.

The timing of resolution
Should be determined with care,
And not unjustly chosen
Because one or the other is unfair.

Discussions must be respectful,
With no personal attacks;
Allow no ridicule or mockery,
But only the true facts.

One must quietly listen
While the other states his case;
Neither is allowed to withdraw
　But engage face to face.

The tunnel may seem endless
And only darkness appears to be,
But remember God is present
And by Him you can still see.

Whatever may be the problem,
He is the answer for you.
If His way is sought out,
He'll show you what to do.

Obstruction will only surface
If one or both won't yield;
In such a case then,
There'll be a deadlock still.

So consider your ways
And truly desire what's right,
Then your conflict will be resolved
As God reveals His light.

Part Eleven

For Men Only: Help for Understanding Your Wife

Husbands, love your wives—be affectionate and sympathetic with them---and do not be harsh or bitter or resentful toward them.

He, who loves his own wife, loves himself. For no one ever hated his own body, but loves it and nourishes and carefully protects and cherishes it, as Christ does the church. (Colossians 3:19; Ephesians 5:25a, 28b, 29, Amp)

…Husbands must give honor to your wives. Treat her with understanding as you live together. She may be weaker than you are, but she is your equal partner in God's gift of new life. If you don't treat her as you should, your prayers will not be heard. (I Peter 3:7, NLT)

The marriage bed should be a place of mutuality – the husband seeking to satisfy his wife, the wife seeking to satisfy her husband. Marriage is not a place to "stand up for your rights." Marriage is a decision to serve the other, whether in bed or not. (I Corinthians 7:4, 5, Msg)

Pleasant words are as an honeycomb, sweet to the soul, and health to the bones. (Proverbs 16:24, KJV)

Value Your Wife

Man is God's highest creation
And for him He has a great plan.
His will for him and his companion
Is to walk hand in hand.

Your assignment as a husband
Is unfailing love for your wife;
Allow bitterness no place
Through any disharmony or strife.

This requires much discipline,
Which is developed from the
  Word.
It may well defy
All the things you've heard.

But to get God's best,
The same is required of you too.
In the end your benefits
Out weigh anything given by you.

The treatment of your wife,
You must give an account of,
And your grade on the test
Depends upon your love.

Since love seeks not her own,
Then this must be true of you too.
So consider your wife first
In all the things that you do

You must care enough to probe
And make it your personal quest.
Until you've exhausted all,
You have not done your best.

Determine her true worth
By what the Bible has said:
For she is more precious than
  rubies
And is a crown for your head.

If she appears locked up,
Keep trying the love key.
For if you persevere,
You'll make it eventually.

Viola T. Miller

Your Image as a Husband

How does your spouse see you
In the secret of her mind?
Are you consistently patient,
And are you always kind?

Have you given notice,
To all that she's done,
In adapting her life to yours,
To form with you a bond?

Do you express appreciation
For sacrifices made for you?
Have you shown gratitude
For all that she's gone through?

Have you taken it for granted
That she placed her life on hold,
To support you and the children
And help you reach your goal?

Have things ever changed,
Or, are they the same way?
Are you bestowing upon her
  honor,
By what you do and say?

Has your life been wonderful,
As you've experienced success?
How much have you
  contributed
To your wife's happiness.

When she reflects back
And thinks over her past,
Have you made it difficult
For the marriage to last?

If it's true in any case
And you've made it so,
Redeem yourself today:
Confess and let her know.

Acknowledge any selfishness,
Any greed or neglect.
Has there been calloused
  unkindness
Or any failure to protect?

If that was not the case,
Then you can be glad,
For your image is positive
For the life that you've had.

Wives Have Special Needs

Husbands often show interest
For their special event,
And at all other times
Very little from them is sent.

But wives need affirmation,
And it's constant each day.
They have need for kindness
That's shown in every way.

They need special support,
When facing a difficult task.
Even though it may be great,
Often they won't ask.

They need to be preferred
Where others are concerned.
They expect loving honor
Which they feel they've earned.

They need to be understood
When they're feeling low,
And assurance that they're okay,
When their blues don't seem to go.

When allowances are made,
And they're able to pull through,
Then behind those days,
They'll make it up to you.

So, give them what they need
And they will compensate.
Then in your times of need,
You won't have to wait.

Viola T. Miller

Free Your Wife

Though your wife won't mention it,
Yet she is still aware.
She knows your resentment
Of her time in prayer.

Whatever she does for God
Will always prove good,
So why not encourage her along
As you know you should.

If you ignore or stifle her
And try to hold her back,
Only you, in the process,
Will experience the lack.

By trying to suppress her
So she can't outshine you,
Only makes her light shine brighter
When it does break through.

There's no need to fear her abilities
Or the gifts she has brought;
Let the whole home benefit
From things she's been taught.

If you allow envy a place,
It will only cloud your mind,
And a pure word from God,
You'll not be able to find.

Binding someone else
Only entraps you too;
So, free your wife completely
To do what God says do.

The Building Blocks to a Strong Marriage

> Remember your assignment
> To love and cherish her.
> Even so, in godliness too,
> May you to her defer.

Viola T. Miller

From A Wife's Perspective

The small things mean a lot,
Much more than husbands know.
It's up to the wives
That they tell them so.

Husbands may think it trivial,
Not worthy of any mention,
But it's in those very things
That wives desire attention.

Though great gifts are appreciated
And much to be desired,
Still they mean much less
When wives don't feel admired.

Their self-esteem is assaulted
When rejected for something said,
Or when there's disagreement,
Yet the husband proceeds ahead.

When they share from their heart
And their husbands appear bored,
That soon diverts attention
To where it's not ignored.

Before long resentment sets in
And it all came to be,
When each denied repeatedly
What was plain to see.

What is the answer then?
What can be done?
Is there assurance for help,
So that the battle is won?

Each must be willing to give,
And both must be willing to take.
By agreeing to compromise,
All works for peace sake.

By each one's willingness
To go the extra mile,
Both learn to trust God
To be there all the while.

Different Construction

Women aren't like microwaves
But more like a crock pot.
If the current is continuous,
It eventually will get hot.

A man of great wisdom
Will accept and understand,
That a woman is uniquely wired
And much different from a man.

Harsh words go down deeply,
And they tend to linger there.
They seldom go away,
Except through much prayer.

Her emotions are fragile
And so quickly bend.
Injured feeling hide themselves,
And they're hard to mend.

Wives are unpredictable,
And are ever so complex;
This is especially so
With issues dealing with sex.

To her it's not just an act
But rather a beautiful season.
Many of her expectations
May extend beyond reason.

Priorities given before
And post actions shown
Will promote greater responses
Than you've ever known.

Viola T. Miller

Time invested wisely
Yields a great dividend.
It will be worth it
To experience a sublime end.

The Threat of Loneliness

What's filling your time
So that attention can't be gained?
Is it that important
That you are entertained?

Shouldn't you be willing
Sometimes to share,
In order to communicate
That you really do care?

Most women need to talk,
So try to understand;
It's more a part of them
Than it is for a man.

If you will not listen,
They will find a way,
For they have that need
To talk about their day.

If a husband goes to his corner
And leaves his wife neglected,
She could experience loneliness,
And feel that she's rejected.

Why should she suffer loneliness,
When her husband is in the house?
Didn't he make her a promise
To be a loving spouse?

Should she feel forsaken,
That she's being replaced?
Whether real or imagined,
The problem must be faced?

She hopes for conversation,
Perhaps a word or two,
But instead for weeks,
There's little or nothing from you.

From one night to another
And for days without end,
She may struggle with the problem
As if she had no friend.

What was your promise,
When you took her hand?
Was it not you'd always
By her side stand?

As she ponders in mind
If there's something she must do,
She is constantly hopeful
That you will come through.

It is your decision
To break through your shell,
And not allow loneliness
To cause your marriage to fail.

Viola T. Miller

Overcoming Myths

Women who're inhibited
Are often labeled "frigid."
But they're not responsible
For backgrounds that were rigid.

Thoughts of sexual freedom
Are associated with lust.
Those misinformed women
Tolerate it in disgust.

But it need not be hopeless
Because there is help in the Word
For those who'll reject
The myths that they've heard.

Patience is most important,
And understanding is the key.
Affection can melt the ice
And help her to be free.

By initiating intimate conversation
As to why little response,
Fears could be dispelled,
And change could come at once.

Counseling could be an aid,
Though it involves risk.
Trusting God for wisdom
Will help you to assist.

By faith all things are possible;
God knows what's going on;
And He'll be there to help
So you'll not go it alone.

The Building Blocks to a Strong Marriage

> Godly knowledge and understanding
> Can accomplish beyond measure.
> When properly dispensed in love,
> It could yield untold pleasure.

Part Twelve

For Men Only: Listen To Your Wife

He who answers before listening-that is his folly and his shame. Love is patient, love is kind…it is not rude… it is not self-seeking. (Proverbs 18:13; I Corinthians 13:4a, 5a, NIV)

Enjoy the wife you married as a young man! Lovely as an angel, beautiful as a rose-don't ever quit taking delight in her body. Never take her for granted. (Proverbs 5:15, Msg)

My fair and beautiful lover-come to me! Come, my shy and modest dove-Leave your seclusion, come out in the open. Let me see your face, let me hear your voice. For your voice is soothing and your face is ravishing.
Kiss me again and again, for your love is sweeter than wine. (Song of Solomon 2:14, Msg; 1:2, TLB)

Fools think they need no advice, but the wise listen to others. (Proverbs 12:15, NLT)

Listen and Learn

Listen to your wife;
Don't go on what you've heard.
What you think is true
May be to her absurd.

Listening promotes communion
And prevents undue stress.
It communicates worth
As it lays fears to rest.

Your wife knows what pleases her
Which may be weird in your sight,
But to ignore her continually
Will cause an emotional fight.

Remember you two are different,
And you're not in her head.
Take her instructions to heart
And not what you think instead.

Don't pretend you know
For it only builds a wall,
Which is so often responsible
For causing a marriage to fall.

She may continue to go along
And nothing may be said,
But just remember the fact
She's going by her head.

If she's anyway upset,
Emotionally, she's on reject,
And she unconsciously feels
Herself, she must protect.

Though women are complex,
Yet knowledge of them is near,
And it becomes accessible
To husbands who will hear.

Both spouses can benefit
By a willingness to learn,
When each seeks the other's good
Out of a genuine concern.

As love is communicated,
The same will be given to you,
And soon the effect will be
  obvious
In all that you want it to.

Fulfillment can be a reality
When pride's not in the way,
As each listens attentively
To what the other has to say.

Viola T. Miller

She Feels Neglected

It may mean nothing to you,
Her mind may not seem sound,
But it means the world to her,
When you don't put her down.

Sure, she has peculiarities,
Many of which, you don't know
Because she keeps them hidden,
Not daring to let them show.

Too often she is searching,
Hoping to find some outlet,
One she can share with fully
Beyond boundaries you've set.

You may be the source
Of her wondering what to do,
Because there's so little interest
Coming to her from you.

It may well be logical
When you have nothing to say,
But it doesn't lessen the pain;
It hurts down deep anyway.

So she tries talking to the kids
Or goes on a shopping spree,
But what good are pretty clothes
If you never seem to see.

The issue must be addressed,
So don't allow it to go on.
Stop neglecting your wife
And leaving her on her own.

Idleness only breeds trouble,
And it's not far ahead
When husbands are insensitive
And won't listen to what's said.

Viola T. Miller

Why She Has No Interest

It's hard to be interested
And to willingly yield,
When consideration is not given
To the way that she feels.

It's hard to be cooperative
When she feels that she's ignored
And when it's brought to attention,
You merely appear bored.

If you tried placing yourself
Where she seems to be,
Then you'd understand
What she seems to see.

It's hard to be responsive
When affection is not displayed.
Though she works with her emotions,
Still they are not swayed.

She must know you're concerned,
And feel that you care,
And be totally convinced,
That you are always there.

If love were purely expressed
Without sex in view,
Yielding would be spontaneous
With eager response to you.

There is always hope
If you're willing to understand
As you seek each other's help
In learning all you can.

The Building Blocks to a Strong Marriage

Help Her Not to Freeze

She needs you to listen
To what she says to you
Though you mean well
By all that you do.

She needs time for love
So don't rush her please.
That has been the problem
Which caused her to freeze.

You need to be sweet
In word and in deed.
Those are precious jewels
That all women need.

You need to invest tenderness,
And kind, loving acts,
And listen with interest
As she relays the facts.

It may not make sense
But still you will see
During intimate times,
How yielded she can be.

If any situations arises
Where something negative is said,
Emotions will remember it
When you are in bed.

If problems aren't taken care of
When she is offended,
The whole act falls short
Of what was intended.

So what can you do
And what can you say?
First submit to God
And He'll reveal the way.

Viola T. Miller

Identifying What She Likes

She likes it when you go places
And don't rush her about,
But instead show love and
  patience
When you take her out.

She likes it when all is laid aside
And everything is great,
When you forget about everything
And take her on a date.

She likes it immensely
When you side with what's true
And though you're proved wrong,
Integrity means more to you.

She likes it when you help out,
Seeing there's too much to do,
So you just step right up
Without being asked to.

She likes it when you cheer her
Though you're also down
And you stay near her
Because you're needed around.

She likes it when you just listen
As you hear her information,
Yet there's no volunteering
To give your explanation.

She likes it when you cooperate
With what she desires to do,
Even though at the time
You may not want to.

Your motivation to excellence
Is just what she needs
To persevere in her endeavors
Until she succeeds.

Part Thirteen

For Women Only: Help for Understanding Your Husband

...Only the Lord can give an understanding wife. (Proverbs 19:14b, NLT)

An anxious heart weighs a man down, but a kind word cheers him up. (Proverbs 12:25, NIV)

In everything you do, stay away from complaining and arguing. (Philippians 2:14, NLT)

The wife's body does not belong to her alone, but also to her husband. In the same way, the husband's body does not belong to him alone, but also to his wife.
Do not deprive each other except for mutual consent and for a time so that you may devote yourselves to prayer. Then come together again so that Satan cannot tempt you because of your lack of self-control. (I Corinthians 7:4, 5, NIV)

Viola T. Miller

Your Image as a Wife

How are you perceived
In your husband's eyes?
When it comes to attending him,
Does he think you compromise?

Do you show him patience,
Having a good attitude?
Does he often have to cope
With you in a bad mood?

Do you seldom talk to him
In general conversation
But freely talk to others
And have no reservation?

Do you often affirm him,
Verbalizing what he means?
Do you often defer to him,
To fulfill his dreams?

Are you easy to get along with,
Seeking to be his dream wife?

Does he consider you a blessing,
An inspiration to his life?

Do you make yourself attractive,
Caring how you appear?
Are you responsive to his
  affections,
Whenever he comes near?

Do you take him for granted,
Expecting him to come through,
Yet very little cooperation
Comes to him from you?

When he does something special,
Do you make it a big deal,
Or do you just ignore it,
Never expressing how you feel?

As you reflect on how it's been,
And you are not satisfied,
Make the changes necessary
And don't let them be denied.

The Building Blocks to a Strong Marriage

Stop Complaining

Before you start complaining,
First just think on this:
If you didn't have your spouse,
What would you stand to miss?

Before you were married,
Were there flaws to see?
Did you complain then
Or hoped they'd flee?

They didn't go away
And now them, you can't ignore.
Instead of them diminishing
It seems that there're more.

Whatever appeared in courtship
Was a sample of the best;
If it went unchallenged then,
You were guaranteed the rest.

To make the best of everything
You must change your thinking.
It'll be your survival kit
To keep your boat from sinking.

Enumerate the positive points.
Accentuate your mate's good.
It will motivate him/her
To do the things he/she should.

Complaining is a negative trait;
Determine to give it no voice.
Drawing from power within
Will be a better choice.

Have a thankful heart,
And think how bad it could be;
You may not have everything,
But there's plenty of good to see.

Viola T. Miller

Cut the Chatter

If you talk too much,
It will soon be resented.
Try listening without comment
To all that is presented.

Wisdom watches her words
And guards all their content,
Considering the hearts and lives
Into whom they're sent.

Watch your delivery,
For it could derail it all,
Causing heaviness on the ear
Of him to whom you call.

The time to speak is crucial
For if it is misplaced,
No solution will ever come
To any problem that's faced.

The advice may be invaluable,
Something that's really good,
But the lack of sensitivity
Won't let it be understood.

The place is just as crucial,
As well as who's around.
Be careful that the intent
Indeed matches the sound.

Words carefully chosen
Form a beautiful mold.
When they're received,
Wisdom can then unfold.

As water reflects one's face,
So words reflect one's heart.
When they are edifying,
Unity does its part.

So watch whatever you say
And let your words be few,
Then your mate will be pleased
To converse with you.

The Building Blocks to a Strong Marriage

Be Informed About Men

Because of their makeup,
Men can instantly be on go;
This is an important fact,
Which every wife should know.

As for as she's concerned,
Close cuddling may very well do
But to a man's body
That means you're ready too.

It takes determined discipline
For him to manage control,
And read actions correctly
Even after he's been told.

Satan plays upon ignorance,
When women don't understand.
He uses it for his benefit
To deceive wherever he can.

Sex was designed by God,
And is really strong in man.
Though he's totally committed,
It takes his all to stand.

Marriage is God's provision
For this need to be satisfied.
A wise understanding spouse
Will see that it's not denied.

Perception of this powerful force
And realizing what's at stake,
A discerning wife educates herself
For her own sake.

Men are mostly visual;
This is known by the Adversary.
He gives them plenty to look at
Because response is involuntary.

Once a thought hits his brain,
He will not have to fret,
When he has a shield- reminder:
"My needs are already met."

Viola T. Miller

Understanding Men

A man is generally private
And keeps his feelings inside.
Though he's deeply affected,
Himself, he tends to hide.

He often finds it difficult
To say just what he intends,
And his means of expression
Often unintentionally offends.

He's more willing to listen
When approached in a kind way,
For he is not influenced
When he's pressured night and day.

Nagging is not the answer
When silence is his choice.
Though you may feel impatient,
Just refuse to give it voice.

He may love you ever so deeply
And yet not voice it to you,
For to him words aren't as important
As what you say or do.

Be cautious not to condemn him
Though you do not understand.
Remember that his behavior
May be peculiarity of a man.

Through much seeking in prayer
And with wisdom from above,
Wives can understand their husbands
And conquer them by love.

You have two ears to listen
And one mouth to speak.
So listen twice as much
When emotions reach a peak.

Men will often speak
Without saying a word.
A response may not be given
Yet you know they've heard.

Give them the time needed
And let them sort things out.
Resist every temptation
That provokes you to pout.

Men seldom handle things
The way women want them to.
They don't solve problems
The way that women do.

Ask God how to relate,
When something is affecting you.
Remember you can't change him
No matter what you do.

Your change in attitude
Can have a great impact,
And it can do much more
Than any kind of attack.

Communication Relieves Frustration

It should be kept in mind
Your partner isn't in your head,
So don't count on his reading your thoughts.
Just make them known instead.

Usually men are sexually aggressive ,
But occasionally hesitation is shown.
Wives need not suffer in silence;
They can let their wishes be known.

Sex should never be used as a weapon
By either a husband or wife;
Nor should it in any way
Cause frustration in either one's life.

To threaten or punish by it
Was never God's aim,
Nor was it to be exploited
Or be for negative gain.

The Bible clearly declares
Your body is your spouse's too,
And neither is to refuse the other
Just because he/she chooses to.

There will be occasions
When there is need to decline,
But it should be reasonable,
Not any excuse you can find.

Differences in personal preferences
Or in frequency of accommodation
Should find their negotiation
Through loving communication.

Refusal should never come over
In a moody, hostile way,
And love should make allowances
And know when to delay.

Neither one should feel cheated
Or have feelings of being rejected;
When unselfish love is communicated,
Then both will feel respected.

Part Fourteen

For Women Only: Listen to Your Husband

Be beautiful inside, in your hearts, with the lasting charm of a gentle and quiet sprit that is so precious to God. (I Peter 3:4, TLB)

When a good man speaks, he is worth listening to… (Proverbs 10:20, TLB)

A wise man's words express deep streams of thought. (Proverbs 18:4, TLB).

A nagging wife is as annoying as a constant dripping on a rainy day.
Don't talk too much; it fosters sin. Be sensible and turn off the flow.
It is better to live alone in the in the desert than with a crabby, complaining wife. (Proverbs 10:19; 27:15; 21:19, NLT)

Give Him Some Space

Nothing is wrong with him
Because he wants a little space;
He needs some sorting time
Concerning the problems he'll face.

It has nothing to do with you
So don't assume that he's mad.
Everything is all right with him
Even though he may appear sad.

He needs some time alone
With the war that's in his mind.
Let him wrestle if he chooses,
The answer he'll soon find.

When he feels it is over,
Then he'll convey it to you,
But until then it's not clear,
So let him work it through.

He doesn't solve things as you do,
So just let him be a man,
And he'll try to be civil
In every way that he can.

When God made men
He decided the plan.
He made women one way
And another He made man.

Yet by their differences
Together they make a whole,
As they join together willingly
In singleness of heart and soul.

Viola T. Miller

Are You the Cause?

A husband needs to always know
He has a wife who will understand.
Especially if he fails,
When he does the best he can.

If he feels everything he does
Will only causes debate,
He'll hesitate to do anything,
For fear you will aggravate.

If he is not fully assured
That something'll be appreciated,
Then the feeling of inadequacy
Will cause him to be frustrated.

If his best is not enough,
He doesn't have anything left.
At most he only feels defeat
And not very sure of himself.

When asked to interact with you,
He may have nothing to say.
His reason often being,
"What's the use any way."

If he decides to speak up,
He can barely get out a bit
Before you cut him off
And then you finish it.

When he tries to find a way
And hopes it will satisfy,
He needs you to accept it
Or he won't continue to try.

With every negative situation,
He experiences erosion.
This must be stopped
Before there is an explosion.

God is willing to help
If you'll allow him to.
Through prayer and supplication
You can find out what to do.

Viola T. Miller

Listen More, Talk Less

If one answers before listening,
To him it is not wise,
Though it may seem good
And harmless in his/her eyes.

This sabotages what's said
And strife is given space;
Communication is cut off,
And Satan has a place.

Each has the exhortation:
Be ready to quickly hear,
Think before speaking
And never close your ear.

Try being still while listening
Instead of moving about,
Practice keeping your focus
As you hear each other out.

It may be difficult at times,
Yet it's possible to learn,
And by willing sacrifice
Loving respect you'll learn.

Though you're tempted to speak,
Just listen intensely instead;
Allow your partner to finish
Before you go on ahead.

The more you practice listening
The greater your intimacy;
For it communicates love
For each of you mutually.

Each time a victory is scored
Division will suffer defeat,
Unity will be promoted,
And Satan will lose his seat.

At first, it may seem useless,
But be assured it's not lost.
There is hope in every situation,
But it comes with a cost.

God is ever so patient,
As He listens to all.
May we follow His example
Whenever our mates call.

What I Like About You

I Like it when you help me
In all the ways you do
And never draw attention
To it coming from you.

I like the encouragement you give
When I'm feeling down,
And you know what to say
When you come around.

I like your understanding
When I make a mistake,
And you straighten it out,
Yet no credit you take.

I like it when you under gird me,
Always doing your best
And when something confronts me,
Together we pass the test.

I like your standing with me
When I've done my best,
And though it's not enough,
You never treat me less.

You inspire me continually
To do more than I'd ever do,
Because of diligence I can see
Manifesting itself in you.

I count myself to be special
When you heap upon me attention;
And though I've blown it badly,
That, you don't bother to mention.

You inspire me to improve
By your tolerance and attitude,
As you remain pleasant
And not be in a bad mood.

I am grateful to you
Because you won't let me lag;
Though you quietly persist,
Yet you don't nag.

I feel your loving care
As you do all that you can
To promote my self-esteem
And motivate me as a man.

I feel like I'm a king
When I am admired
And you come on to me
Because I am desired.

I know that I am blessed,
And I'm favored from above
Because I've been graced
To be the recipient of your love.

You bring out the best in me;
Words can't express what I mean,
But I hope I prove by my actions
That you are my reigning queen.

Part Fifteen

Hindrances to a Strong Marriage

Don't be selfish; don't live to make a good impression on others. Be humble, thinking of others as better than yourself. (Philippians 2:3, NLT)

Beginning a quarrel is like opening a floodgate, so drop the matter before a dispute breaks out. (Proverbs 17:14, NLT)

Be faithful and true to your wife… A man must love his wife as a part of himself; and the wife must see to it that she deeply respects her husband—obeying, praising and honoring him. (Proverbs 5:15b; Ephesians 5:33, TLB).

Honor Christ by submitting to each other.
You wives must submit to your husband's leadership in the same way you submit to the Lord. (Ephesians 5:21, 22, TLB)

If you are angry, don't sin by nursing your grudge. Don't let the sun go down with you still angry—get over it quickly. For when you are angry, you give a mighty foothold to the devil. (Ephesians 4:26, 27, TLB)

Be gentle, ready to forgive; never hold grudges. Remember the Lord forgave you, so you must forgive others. (Colossians 3:13, TLB)

Pursuit of Wealth Instead of God

When God is given priority
And not accumulation of wealth,
It'll be granted in the process
Along with joy, peace and health.

For all who set themselves
To make riches their aim
Will only find emptiness
And not receive their claim.

It is not within a man
To direct his own way;
Try it if you'd like
And do whatever you may.

Without God's knowledge
Wrong will appear right,
And the true value of things
Will be an oversight.

To think the quality of life
Depends upon one's wealth
Will prove to be deception
And weaken marital health.

All the energy employed
Will be discovered waste,
As it will prove worthless
To pursue riches in haste.

What does it benefit
If one gains the whole world,
But yet he misses Heaven
And into Hell be hurled.

What happens after this life
Dictates the perspective of worth
And commands one's focus
During life's time on earth.

Constantly pursuing wealth
While God aside is laid
Will prove fruitless in the end,
If eternal provisions aren't made.

The length of a human life
Has a specific measure
And one's eternal preparation
Has an eternal treasure.

God made provisions for all
And will bestow riches in life
When He is given place
In the life of a husband and wife.

Upon everyone's life,
There is a definite call,
But it will only be realized
When Christ is Lord of all.

Viola T. Miller

Strife Destroys

Strife is a number one killer,
And it is sent to destroy.
It uses various schemes,
Its poison to employ.

It stems from opposition
Commencing in the head,
And conceives some additions
To anything that's said.

It instigates secret wars
Before the battle cry,
By causing fruitless quarrels
And neither one knows why.

When a struggle presents itself,
Someone must understand:
If the argument isn't diffused,
It's destined to get out of hand.

Words may be released
Which neither one really means

And some one needs to perceive
It isn't as bad as it seems.

Strife has an evil nature
Which endeavor's to persist.
If a couple is wise enough
It's destruction they'll resist.

God will supply the help
And give power from within,
When there's genuine desire
To be free of the sin.

Before strife is encountered
There should be a plan;
The plan is for disarmament
Which both understand.

When only the issue is addressed
And response is to it alone,
Words against each other
Will not destroy the home.

Controlling Anger

Examine the source of anger
And find the cause of frustrations.
See if the negative eruptions
Stemmed from past situations.

When the source is located
And acknowledged as being there,
Then one is in position
To extinguish the flare.

Only fools vent their anger,
Not regarding what is said,
As they speak with no discernment,
Being emotionally led.

Because one's mate is valuable,
And both care how the other feels,
When there're anger outbursts,
Caution should employ seals.

Since words can hurt so deeply,
There should be constant care,
So that diligence is always taken
To not speak out in despair.

By keeping hearts securely,
Couples set watch over their lives,
And they guard the fellowship
Enjoyed as husbands and wives.

Especially with feelings of pressure,
Must they be on the alert
And take care in speaking to each other
So that neither spews words of hurt.

Viola T. Miller

Fear Weakens Relationships

Fear is that uneasy feeling,
A sense that all is not well.
It's that which induces worry
Or concern that one might fail.

It's a sense of inadequacy
Which you feel you must hide
As it steals your security
And your peace deep inside.

It's a feeling of apprehension
That there's danger up ahead,
And it controls your actions
Though nothing has been said.

Fear is a tormentor,
As it works in disguise.
It trips up contented couples,
Who have not yet become wise.

When fear is given a place,
It'll find a way to reign.
Until it is withstood,
Peace, you'll not regain.

There will be uncertainty
Or pressure to rush right in,
Though you're not convinced
That a project should begin?

As fear causes uneasiness
And places peace on pause,
Soon there's suspicion of evil
When there is no cause.

There'll be mistrust and accusation
Though clearly all is right.
You'll constantly be suspicious
When you're out of sight.

Fear is Satan's instrument;
He uses it to bring up your past.
His aim is to steal, kill or destroy
So that your relationship won't last.

God does not send fear,
For He gives only peace.
As trust is placed in Him,
Fear will eventually cease.

So stand up against it inside
And resist temptation's demand.
Then in love, joy and peace
You will begin to stand.

The Building Blocks to a Strong Marriage

Plea Against Stubbornness

You have shut me out
When I've tried talking to you.
Do you have any idea,
What something like that can do?

No matter what I've tried,
It seems I've been rejected;
If you'd only listen to me,
At least I would feel respected.

Before we were married
We only dreamed of bliss;
What has gone so wrong
That we've come to this?

Why must you constantly
Pick everything apart?
Have you ever considered
How that breaks my heart?

Whatever the issues are,
Shouldn't we both know?
Then we could deal with them
So all this tension could go.

What was it anyway?
What pulled us apart?
It can't be as great
As the love within our heart.

Whatever the cause might be
I will take the blame,
For when something's between us
Nothing is the same.

I have tried eating
But my food isn't right;
I have tried resting,
But I can't sleep at night.

I've tried to think,
But my mind won't go;
I've tried to function
But I forget what I know.

I've missed you so much,
Though you've been near;
But we've seemed miles apart
As though you weren't here.

I want to see your smile
And feel your embrace;
Another lonely night like this,
I just cannot face.

What must I do
To show how much I care?
If you'll just name it,
I will see that it's there.

Viola T. Miller

Unforgiveness Blocks

Unforgiveness is a great hindrance
Which holds its captives fast.
It robs them of peace
And keeps them in the past.

It holds its owners down
Keeping them tightly bound,
Affecting them adversely
And all that are around.

As it spills its poison
All fellowship ceases.
Though motions may continue,
All communication freezes.

Very little will be accomplished
For upon nothing you'll agree;
Each remains paralyzed
And no one can go free.

Only God can make it right
When to Him both pray.
He alone can conquer all
And show both the way.

If a grudge is held,
Forgetting about the Word,
Prayers that are uttered
Won't be answered or heard.

What should be the verdict ,
Concerning a past scar?
Forgiveness is the best choice
To move from where you are.

By making the decision
To forgive in Jesus' name,
God's power can be trusted
To eradicate the claim.

Granting undeserved pardon
And mercy to be received,
Will set the holder free
Even if still grieved.

When this is enforced
And is considered past,
God can grant grace
And hurt will not last.

The Building Blocks to a Strong Marriage

Unwise Phrases

Refuse to be an accuser
Though opportunity will be there.
Choose to pass it up anyway
If you really care.

Never ridicule the partner
Who caused what was done,
He/she needs no reminder
To know who's the one.

Forbearance is a better route;
Understanding is a superior way.
Both will inspire harmony
More than words can say.

Avoid saying "You always,"
For it's mere exaggeration,
Mostly uncontrolled outburst
From an inward frustration.

Avoid saying, "Why can't you,"
For it causes emotional stir,
And this will easily degenerate
Into a provocative slur.

Avoid saying, "That's it,"
For finality closes the door,
While patience keeps it open
And leaves room for more.

Avoid asking, "Now what is it?"
For it'll only cause strife,
And there's no need to give place
To negatives in your life.

Avoid saying, "I can't believe you've,"
For it has a negative sound,
And it points subtly
At some fault that you've found.

Try to avoid sighing
For it implies you're upset;
If it becomes habitual,
The same by you will be met.

These phrases breed disharmony,
And they are hard to undo;
So be ever so careful
About messages sent from you.

There is always a tactful way
To say what you mean.
God is willing to give you skill
When you upon Him lean.

Part Sixteen

Abuse Revealed

The Lord is close to the broken hearted; He rescues those who are crushed in spirit. (Psalms 34:18, NLT)

Give your burdens to the Lord, and He will take care of you. He will not allow the godly to slip and fall. (Psalms 55:20, NLT)

Reckless words pierce like a sword, but the tongue of the wise brings healing. (Proverbs 12:18, NIV)

What time I am Afraid I will trust in thee. (Psalms 56:3, KJV)

Recognizing Abuse

Abuse is being mistreated
In either word or deed.
It is to be unacceptable
So never give it heed.

It may be somewhat subtle
Through expressions that are sent,
And it can be recognized,
That hurt was its intent.

It may be spousal control,
Not allowing you to be free.
Even if it's not spoken,
The attitude you can see.

If you're constantly being rejected
And often falsely accused,
The intent of suffering is there;
You are clearly being abused.

It may take the form of criticism
Or a constant put down,
Implying by word or action
That your mind is unsound.

It may take the form of threats
And daring you to tell

Or uncontrolled fits of anger
When you've not done something well.

It may be any form of mistreatment
Where you feel oppression
Or any form of degrading
Where you're treated as a possession.

It may be a push, a grab or snatch
When you don't comply.
It may be through twisting your words
Into a concocted lie.

It may be controlling assets
Or threatening to give you less;
It may be stressful rejection
Causing you to find no rest.

If by any means you are hurt,
Or you are being confused,
Then it is for certain,
You are being abused.

Viola T. Miller

Am I Abusive?

Am I an abusive person
By the things that I say?
Do I often become violent
When things don't go my way?

Do I speak unadvisedly
For no reason at all?
Must I have immediate movement
When I sound a call.

When there is no compliance,
What happens in my mind?
Do I become someone else
Who speaks or acts unkind?

Do I demand spousal agreement,
Even though I am wrong?
Do I feel no conscience
When he or she goes along?

Do I hurt people I love,
Though I don't want to?
Yet, it happens anyway
And there is nothing I can do?

When it passes over
Do I feel terribly sad,
That something so trivial
Could make me so mad?

Do I need help myself
That I hurt not another's life?
If my answer indeed is yes,
I'm an abusive husband or wife.

The Building Blocks to a Strong Marriage

Submission Myths

Submission is not silence
Or appearing to be dead.
It isn't being stupid
And not using your head.

It isn't swallowing everything
Or just being a doormat;
It isn't being passive
From intellectual lack.

It's not hoping that you'll float
Though you feel that you're
  sinking,
Yet you abdicate to your spouse
All of your independent thinking.

Submission is not being ignorant
As if you've not been taught;
It's not being as a slave
Whom a master has bought.

It isn't cowering under,
Hoping to win yourself love;
It isn't staying down beneath
And never immerging above.

It isn't waiting for permission
Or you will never go.
It's not fearing to improve
  yourself,
Unless you're told to do so.

Submission is not being penniless
With no money to hold,

Dependent upon your spouse
Because of his/her obvious
  control.

It's not being oppressed,
And taking it for peace's sake;
It isn't experiencing fear
Every morning when you awake.

Submission is not being quiet
When you don't agree;
It's not being a coward
Because you're not free.

It's not losing your identity
As though you don't exist,
And becoming someone else
Because your spouse insists.

It isn't always giving in
In order to have peace;
It isn't always keeping quiet
Hoping arguments will cease.

Submission isn't tipping around
As if walking on shells,
Because when you refuse,
Your spouse always yells.

Submission is not jumping as high
As your spouse might demand,
Because you feel you must
To receive a helping hand.

Viola T. Miller

It is not silently suffering
Though you feel you're used.
It's not accepting as fate
Being physically abused.

None were created that way,
For God made it clear,
Spouses are to be nurtured
And not to live in fear.

None of this is true
For submission to be enforced.
It's because of this deception
Many have been divorced.

The Scriptures give the blueprint
Which defines God's intent,
When He prescribed submission,
And by it what He meant.

Coping with Low Self-Esteem

What is low self-esteem?
And how does it show?
Is it something detectable?
If so, how can you know?

It can easily be recognized,
And cowering down is one way.
When you are a victim,
You'll have very little to say.

Though you may be dishonored,
You'll receive it from day to day,
As you take whatever is doled out,
And never complain in any way.

It results in taking no thought
Of whatever your needs,
Because you dare not speak out,
Whatever are the deeds.

Low-esteem costs much
As it takes its toll,
Because it never allows freedom
That its victim might unfold.

If you have low esteem for
 yourself,
You can easily assume others wise,
Because intelligence for yourself,
You can only surmise.

You quickly encourage others,
But won't receive it for yourself.

Feeling unworthy to make choices,
You settle for whatever's left.

When you're called to a position
And you refuse to take the place,
Then it spells low-or no esteem,
And that you must face.

When you are mistreated
And you feel obligation to take it,
It's because you deem it necessary
Or you may not be able to make it.

Low esteem is the problem,
For each situation reveals a sign.
Having adapted to its demand,
It doesn't come to mind.

Something has happened
 somewhere
Which has made your perception
 wrong.
But by your will, you can recover
And not allow it to go on.

Knowledge brings deliverance
When it is embraced;
For only then can it dispel for you
Any problem that is faced.

God made you valuable,
So nothing less receive;
And contrary thought to it,
See that you not believe.

Part Seventeen

Dealing with Unsaved Spouses

Wives, fit into your husbands' plans; for if they refuse to listen when you talk to them, about the Lord, they will be won by your respectful, pure behavior. Your godly lives will speak better than any words. (I Peter 1:1, 2, TLB)

... If a Christian has a wife who is not a Christian but she wants to stay with him anyway, he must not leave her or divorce her. And if a Christian woman has a husband who isn't a Christian and he is willing to stay with her, she must not leave him. For perhaps the husband who isn't a Christian may become a Christian with the help of his Christian wife. And the wife, who isn't a Christian, may become a Christian with the help of her Christian husband. Otherwise, if the family separates, the children may never come to know the Lord; whereas a united family may, in God's plan, result in the children's salvation.

But if the husband or wife, who isn't a Christian, is eager to leave, it is permitted.

In such cases, the Christian husband or wife should not insist that the other stay, for God wants His children to live in peace and harmony.

For after all, there's no assurance to you wives that your husband will be converted if you stay; and the same may be said to you husbands concerning your wives. (I Corinthians 7:12-15, TLB)

Place No One Above God

Often believers withdraw from God,
Thinking it'll promote peace,
But when someone is given God's place
The flow of good will cease.

It may appear that peace has come
But at most it'll be temporary,
For it's only a matter of time
Something else will go contrary.

No one is ever required
To deify a man,
And this should be refused
To any order or command.

God must have first place
To experience real success.
If He's positioned anywhere else
Nothing will be at its best.

He has placed a husband
As the head of his house
But not to lord it over
Or intimidate his spouse.

Only being called as the leader
Was his honor meant to be
And not family enthronement
For all around to see.

Though it is a noble goal
To be a loving wife,
It can never be accomplished
Unless God rules a life.

Viola T. Miller

When He has His worthy place
In fellowship and in love,
Then will all else in life
Will be blessed from Him above.

Being an Effective Witness

Is there a clear difference in you
Except for what you say?
Does your Christian profession
Seem to be an attractive way?

Is your faith generally at work
To such distinct degrees
That it motivates your lost spouse
To desire what he/she sees?

Is there a marked distinction
Displayed in every situation
Which proves your faithfulness,
And enhances your relation?

Do you allow the presence of
  Christ
To cause His wisdom to flow,
Instead of your competition
To show what you know?

When there's disagreement,
Is harmony still maintained?
When there's misunderstanding,
Is it by you peace is regained?

Your light will shine brighter
By your willingness in giving;
It is your best testimony
Of the life that you're living.

By continually intimidating
And pointing to your mate's lack,
Your witness becomes resented
And only causes drawback.

Even without a word
Something is being said;
Your quiet abiding faith
Is preaching in your stead.

Your job is not to convict
Or force upon others your way.
God will do the convincing
By what you do or say.

If you were the unbeliever
And your spouse had to deal with
  you,
Would his/her witness be
  powerful enough
To entice you to come through?

By simply abiding quietly,
Much is being said,
And it is more effective
Than loud preaching instead.

By this you can easily see
What really needs to be done,
In order to be an effective witness
And get your lost mate won.

Viola T. Miller

Bridging the Gap

Many problems will arise
And disconnections will come
When two spouses are different
And are not spiritually one.

It may be one is a believer,
While the other is outside,
Or possibly in the same faith,
The two do not abide.

This should've been settled
Long before the vow;
But still it's not impossible
To be conquered somehow.

God doesn't author confusion,
But He creates peace.
And He does the impossible
To cause wars to cease.

He needs the opportunity
Before all else fails,
And he wants to navigate
The direction your boat sails.

Your spouse may challenge you
On something you're to do,
Just to cause some friction
And to place pressure on you.

Pray for strength to be gracious
When you know you're to refuse,
Because you're being tried
In hopes that you may lose.

Never feel you're responsible
And let compromise be your cost;
Neither blame it on yourself,
If your spouse ends up lost.

God will give wisdom
And will help you to do what's right,
Not in a rebellious manner,
But with His calm delight.

There should not be pressure
To make each other conform,
For endeavoring to force change
Will only cause a storm.

It is very important for you
To be cautious on participations.
Being outside the home too often,
Will deteriorate your relations.

It is also very crucial
To maintain a balanced stand
And to concern yourself primarily
With necessities if you can.

Try being as cooperative
As your faith will allow,
And trust God to help you
Live for Him somehow.

Maintain a wonderful attitude,
And let it be on natural display;

The Building Blocks to a Strong Marriage

Whenever something's contrary
Keep trusting in God anyway.

Where intimacy is concerned,
Let there not be any lack
Because that will be occasion
For you to suffer attack.

More freedom will be granted
When prior approval is sought,

Rather than making mention
Only as an afterthought.

Nothing is impossible with God
And to you He'll surely reveal
How to overcome difficulties
While endeavoring to do His will.

Part Eighteen

Recognizing Different Seasons in Life

There is a time for everything, a season for every activity under heaven. (Ecclesiastes 3:1, NLT)

Live happily with the woman you love all the meaningless days of life that God has given you in this world. The wife God gives you is your reward for your earthly toil. (Ecclesiastes 9:9, NLT)

Kind words are like honey—sweet to the soul and healthy for the body. (Proverbs 16:24, NLT)

He fills my life with good things; my youth is renewed like the eagles. (Psalms 103:5, NLT)

Most important of all, continue to show love for each other, for love covers a multitude of sins. (I Peter 4:8, NLT)

Recognizing the Fear of Aging

The fear of aging
Comes before one knows it;
It does its secret work,
Long before one shows it.

It'll manifest itself
And not declare its name,
But because of its fruit,
It's known just the same.

It is easily recognized
Through unnecessary defense,
By unexplained withdrawals,
Which seem to make no sense.

As fear begins to surface,
Frustration gradually shows,
Its victims suffer in silence,
And hope that no one knows.

There's a lack of enthusiasm
And difficulty in concentration,
Which result in isolation
And in seldom participation.

What can be done about it
To restore interest back?
What is really the answer
To this age-old attack?

Knowledge is the answer,
Since the "unknown" breeds fear.
God is willing to help
And He is always near.

As with all development,
Age will cause decline;
But with this realization,
There can be peace of mind.

By anticipating change with age
And having understanding in
 place,
Couples can make allowances
For everything they'll face.

Viola T. Miller

Changes Will Come

No one remains the same
Though we'd all like to,
But age and other things
Will somehow change you.

Knowledge is the key
That unlocks a jammed door,
And keeps a marriage sailing
Instead of docking at shore.

In spite of all ourselves
Our bodies eventually slow down,
And we must work harder
To cover the same ground.

Nothing has to go wrong
And both may do what's right,
There may never be an argument,
And there may never be a fight.

The sun continues to rise
And the moon continues to shine,
But the glimmer of the stars
Seem so hard to find.

What is this madness,
And what gives it birth?
Is it just a phenomenon
All must face on earth?

In the human body,
Eventually functions decrease;
Some of what's voluntary
Actually seem to cease.

But when we are informed
And know what to expect,
Then ignorance of our status
Won't cause us to be upset.

Changes will come to all,
And that we can't control;
But we can age gracefully
As life cycles unfold.

One might feel helpless
And a bit hollow inside;
But the safest thing is sharing it
And not trying to hide.

Frankness is the best policy,
So allow fear no place;
When you choose to work through it,
God will give you the grace.

There's nothing wrong with your mate
And nothing is wrong with you.
As both change life's cycles,
Help to see each other through.

Feed your love more deeply,
And give your mate your best.
Let catering to each other
Be your earnest quest.

Thank God for each other
And appreciate this time in life.
Celebrate the joys left
To share as a husband and wife.

Coping with Menopause (Husbands)

All living things change
So expect it from your mate too.
Much of the ease in transition
Depends largely upon you.

Assuming this to be true,
Be determined to understand.
The first step is a decision
To support all that you can.

There'll be need for the assurance
That you'll always be there;
So you should constantly verbalize
How much that you still care.

When interest and endurance
  change,
They will not be her call.
If it were left to her,
They wouldn't come at all.

Mother Nature is to blame
For doing what she must do.
After her cocoon stage,
A butterfly will come through.

As transition begins to emerge
You'll observe changing moods.
Give to them no mention
Unless to them, she alludes.

When she insists it's hot,
But you know that it's cold,
Just turn on some air;
The truth will soon unfold.

When she contends it's cool
But you know that it's hot,
Turn the heat up anyway
Just as though it's not.

It may seem at times
Everything is going wrong.
Remember it's only temporary,
And it won't last too long.

So, don't listen to Satan's
  deceptions
And the lies he'll tell you.
Some day you'll experience change,
And will need her support too.

Remember the covenant you made
To be there for one another;
It needs to be honored at this time
Much more than any other.

By your love, knowledge and
  patience,
You will make it through
And by leaning upon God for help,
He will impart strength to you.

Viola T. Miller

Coping with Mid-life Crisis (Wives)

A man enjoys his being able
To have all under control
And never facing anything
That will cause him to fold.

Often in his thoughts
A challenge he fears will call,
And the voice of mid-life
May be the strongest one of all.

The assurance that he needs
For this transition in life
Can best come to him
From an understanding wife.

He's still the man you married
And is engaging what he knows.
He's endeavoring to conceal frustration,
And he hopes it never shows.

It may come as accusation,
But just know you're not to blame.
Try making allowances for him,
Knowing things are not the same.

When confidence comes by knowledge,
It can bring about peace,
Then unwelcome storms
Will begin to cease.

Don't bother questioning him
Unless he's ready to talk.
Just remember your promise,
By his side to walk.

For better or for worse
Was your solemn vow,
So endeavor to honor it
As much as he will allow.

Sow seeds of patience
And loving kindness give,
Then expect a golden harvest
From the life you live.

Stay close to him
And increase your loving care.
Show him by increased attention
You will always be there.

Verbalize unfailing love
With profound determination;
God will reward you
For your loving dedication.

Life can still be wonderful,
But it largely depends upon you.
When you use your faith,
God will see you through.

The Building Blocks to a Strong Marriage

Senior Glow

The senior years should be great,
Just what you've dreamed of,
With freedom from cares and
  stress
As you rest secure in your love.

It's easy to secretly think
"My spouse's youth has left."
This will especially be true
If you only think of yourself.

As you look into the mirror,
Do all of your features remain?
Can you do everything efficiently,
Just exactly the same?

How about your stamina?
Do you just lie or sit?
Have you any mobility
That helps to keep you fit? `

Your spouse has spent his or her
  youth
Since becoming your
  husband/wife.
It's been done unreservedly
To enrich yours and the family's
  life.

You became what you are
Because of many prayers.

They were offered in your behalf
Because he or she cares.

Whatever you can see now
Is what your spouse has left
From expending constant energy
In giving of his or herself.

When it comes to negativity,
There should be none,
But only grateful
  acknowledgement
For all that God has done.

He gives us wisdom
That we all might know
The seasons of our lives
Will have their time and go.

By healthy care and supplements
Stamina can stay in tack,
And life can be so wonderful
It will be as if the clock turned
  back.

The mindset is most important
For as we think, so we are.
One can affect his/her limitations,
And the mind has a say in how far.

Viola T. Miller

Maintaining Loving Focus

Because you're both seniors
Doesn't mean you have no life.
Forever you're a husband
Or forever you are a wife.

The vows you made together
Hold as long as you live,
So let nothing come between you
Still, love you can give.

Keep reminding yourself
Till death do you part,
So stay close to each other;
Be sealed in each other's heart.

What you have is cemented.
It's etched in love's stone.
What you have received
Is for you to own.

Age is only symbolic,
And it shows how long it's been
Since you've entered your race
And in spite of it you win.

Only good experiences should be yours
As you seek to do your best.
In maintaining your togetherness
You can lay fears and intrusions to rest.

Though more effort is required
For oneness to be employed,
Yet it is your loving pledge
Forever to be enjoyed.

Part Nineteen

Is There Hope for a Failed Marriage?

Trust in the Lord with all your heart; do not depend on your own understanding. Seek His will in all you do, and He will direct your paths. (Proverbs 3:5, NLT)

I wait quietly before God, for my hope is in Him. (Psalms 62:5, NLT)

...a righteous man may fall seven times and rise again. (Proverbs 24:16)

Most important of all, continue to show love for each other, for love covers a multitude of sins. (I Peter 4:8, NLT)

Love will last forever... (I Corinthians 13:8a, NLT)

Viola T. Miller

Failed Expectations

What did I expect from marriage
That I have not received?
Did I anticipate too much
And feel I've been deceived?

Did I prepare for marriage,
Searching all things out,
Giving attention especially,
To that which I had doubt?

Did I not realize
All that it entailed?
Were my expectations too high
The reason that it failed?

Did I dare not look ahead,
For fear of what I'd see?
Did I think by not doing so
All would continue to be?

What have I not done
In contributing my part?,
What have I cut off
That was present from the start?

Did I anticipate changes,
When it came to social life?
Did I presume no difference,
Upon becoming a husband or
  wife?

Did I expect no reactions,
To my hanging out?

Did I expect coming in late
To cause spousal doubt?

If explanations weren't given me,
Would I be content?
Would I also suspiciously
  question,
Wondering where he or she went?

What did I expect to do,
If things ever went wrong?
Was I just deceived,
Refusing that to think on?

Did I make any allowances,
For crises that might appear,
So I could face them bravely
And triumph over fear?

What about my in-laws?
Did I allow them too much space
And when they went too far,
Consequences, I couldn't face?

Did I understand about children,
The many demands they'd make?
Did I know what little time I'd
  have,
They'd eventually take?

Were there times I was needed,
But I was an absentee spouse,
During things for everyone else
And neglecting my own house?

The Building Blocks to a Strong Marriage

Did I accept unnecessary tasks,
Not taking time for myself?
Did I do too much for others
And had nothing for me left?

Did I expect of my spouse,
Support that wasn't there?

Did I ever voice my thoughts
That my treatment was unfair?

Because I sat by silently
With only an inwardly blame,
I must take partial credit
That my marriage isn't the same.

Viola T. Miller

Afterthought

What are my feelings,
When marriage comes to mind?
Is it something that secretly,
I wish I'd left behind.

Has it been a troubled sea,
One tossing me more and more?
Have I been trying desperately
To make it back to shore?

Have I been disillusioned,
By false expectations?
Did I enter into it,
Enticed by sensation?

Was I moved by chemistry,
Not knowing what it entailed?
May God please help me:
My marriage seems to have failed.

What differently could I've done,
To have secured a right start?

Did I expect everything of my spouse,
And I never did my part?

What was my part anyway?
Or was I ever told?
Have I expected all to remain,
Until change began to unfold?

If I'd known back then
What I know today,
I would have been prepared
For what has come my way.

But it's not too late;
I know God will see me through,
And by His grace and mercy
I'll do what I have to do.

He can take anything
And make it turn out right,
Causing victory to come
For all who'll gives Him their fight.

It's Not Too late

Can I start over again
Though much time has past?
Can I have another chance,
At a marriage that will last?

What if I'm divorced
And feel happiness is lost?
Was restoration for that included,
When Jesus paid the cost?

Surely it must've been covered
Since He paid for all,
So, that gives me another chance
Though I caused the fall.

Can I have a beautiful marriage,
One that's born from above,
Filled with joy and happiness,
Founded and built on love?

Is it really possible?
Can I share a beautiful life
Where I have a wonderful
 husband,
And I am a loving wife?

When God made marriage,
He said that it was good.
He provided the ingredients
For it to function as it should.

Who caused the problem?
Wasn't it Satan back then,
Who successfully tricked Eve
And caused her to sin?

Nothing is changed today;
I must the truth face.
Every marriage can fail
When Satan is given a place.

God started over with man
When Jesus to us was sent,
Providing a second chance
To all who would repent.

So I can begin again
And start out the right way,
By asking God's forgiveness
And obeying him every day.

Viola T. Miller

Overcoming Boredom

Get in touch with yourself
And find what you enjoy.
Give to it your energy
And time to it employ.

Upon your daily arousal
Before you start your day,
Make it your decision
To lift your eyes and pray.

Life is determined by choices,
So its quality is up to you.
If things aren't as you desire,
Then alter the things you do:

Start by being thankful
And take your mind off yourself;
Develop an interest in others
And a very little time will be left.

Enroll in a computer class
And improve yourself on line.
Check the available links
And unlimited options you'll find.

Develop a hobby for yourself
And give thought and energy to it.
Continue to prayerfully search
Until something seems to fit.

Volunteer to help someone in need
And receive from them no pay;
Satisfaction will be your reward
Just knowing you've made their day.

The Building Blocks to a Strong Marriage

Join a community group
Or organize your own.
Soon you'll be so busy
There won't be time alone.

Part Twenty

Overcoming Defeat

I can do everything with the help of Christ who gives me the strength I need. (Philippians 4:13, NLT)

...Let us not get tired of doing what's right, for after a while we will reap a harvest of blessing if we don't get discouraged and give up. (Galatians 6:9, TLB)

Now thanks be unto God, which always causes us to triumph in Christ… (II Corinthians 2:14a, KJV)

Patient endurance is what you need now, so you will continue to do God's will. (Hebrews 10:36, NLT)

Prayer of Desperation

I pause in hopelessness,
For I'm having difficulty
 praying.
I'm searching desperately;
God, do You hear what I'm
 saying?

My heart feels heavy,
For nothing seems to be right.
I feel constantly depressed
From trouble day and night.

Sleep has left my eyes,
And peace has left my mind.
Right thoughts evade me,
And nothing good I find.

My mate can't understand;
I seem all alone.
My emotions are exhausted
And I can only moan.

I am coming to You
And I believe it's true:

You are ready to dispense
Whatever I need from You.

As I come in turmoil,
I really search for rest.
Please give me the answers
To overcome this test.

As I come in faith,
Desiring to really know,
I am confident inside
What's needed, You'll show.

So as I lay before You
And give you my all,
I submit myself completely
To answer your every call.

Till I am delivered,
I will not leave.
You promised all who'd come
Them, You'd receive.

Viola T. Miller

Struggles with Defeat

Defeat knocks on everyone's door,
Especially through a lost goal;
But there can still be hope
That a miracle might unfold.

Though it seems there's no answer,
Holdfast what you've believed.
It may still be on the way
Though yet you've not received.

Your faith may be tested
As you believe the Word;
So refuse to entertain doubt,
And focus not on what you've heard.

If your doors seem to be shut,
Remember there're larger ones out there;
So just keep on believing,
And they'll open up somewhere.

Holdfast to your dream
In the face of apparent despair.
Don't let your faith die,
For your answer is somewhere.

Nothing is impossible with God,
If it is in His will;
But if it's not, you're better off,
And that He will reveal.

So don't accept an unachieved goal
As though it were defeat.
It will all work for good,
And a better one you'll meet.

Replace disappointment with hope
When you've done your best
Because after you've done your part,
God will do the rest.

Viola T. Miller

The Last Straw

In spite of your doing right,
You could still have a test,
One that's hard to pass
Though you do your best.

You could end up with a spouse
Who just won't respond,
One who is selfish
And won't care for any one.

When it comes to filling needs,
There's nothing he/she will do;
You have tried communicating,
But both ears were deaf to you.

During the many times
That you have tried to share,
You have only been ignored
As if you were not there.

You have prayed for strength
And hope to make it through,
But nothing has changed;
It's no better for you.

Divorce hasn't been an option
You've considered in the past,
For you had hoped and prayed
That this marriage would last.

It has now become apparent
Through unacceptable abuse,
Out of all your trying
There really is no use.

The Building Blocks to a Strong Marriage

God has seen everything,
And He knows that you have tried
But all of your attempts
Were emphatically denied.

Just chalk off everything
As a learning experience for you
For there's nothing left now
But to do what you have to.

Viola T. Miller

Be Encouraged

Many times you've missed the mark
And have not been right,
Sometimes what's been said
Has not reflected light.

But when brought to your attention
You've quickly repented.
Receiving constructive rebuke,
You have not resented.

Be confident of who you are,
Not having to be defined.
Don't accept what someone else says
And by it be confined.

Be thankful for who you are,
Grateful to God above,
Knowing that because of Him
You were made in His love.

Let nothing hold you down,
Nor anything keep you back.
As you've done in the past,
Recover from every attack.

Continue striving for the best
And develop in your calling;
God will always be there,
And He'll keep you from falling.

God is for you
So who against you can win,
As you yield to Him
And keep a way from sin?

Decide to be Happy

If couples leave to chance
The quality of their day,
Seldom will it automatically
Turn out the right way.

It takes a definite decision
For every husband and wife,
To experience joy and peace
And have an abundant life.

The cares of the world
Can easily weigh you down
And turn a cheerful smile
Into a dreadful frown.

Each morning before arising,
Fill your mouth with gratitude.
Through enumerating your
  blessing
You'll ward off a bad mood.

Before negativity sets in
Or has anything to say,
Think of the positive things
You will do that day.

If irritability comes along
And tries to claim a spot,
Jump up and get going
As though it did not.

Happiness is a choice,
Which only you can make,
So anything contrary,
Decide not to take.

When your mind is directed
Because of your decision,
The quality of your life
Will come from that vision.

Ask God for help
And you'll accomplish this,
Then His plan for you,
You will never miss.

Viola T. Miller

Salvation Commitment

I know that I am lost,
And I acknowledge it today.
I make no excuses,
I want to find the way.

Lord, I know I'll meet You,
And I must stand alone,
To give account of myself
And I'll be on my own.

I know I'll pay eternally,
If I don't get it right,
So make me clean, I pray,
And righteous in your sight.

I'm ready to change.
I know You paid the cost,
When You died for me
Out there on the cross.

As I understand it,
There is nothing I can do
To make myself right,
Or be worthy of You.

As I come to You a sinner,
Please change my state;
Consequently, my home will be Heaven,
And Hell won't be my fate.

I accept You as my Savior,
As I now upon You I call,
Be my Lord forever,
I give to You my all.

The Building Blocks to a Strong Marriage

About the Author

Viola Miller and her husband, Billy, reside in their hometown of Luxora, Arkansas, which has a population of about 1300 and is located in northeastern Arkansas. Both are retired schoolteachers and are parents of two sons, Billy, Jr and Adrian.

Growing up the sixth of seven siblings, Viola was inspired by her minister father to take an interest in the Bible when she saw him study it so intensely. Having the same pursuit of its knowledge and understanding, her writings have a strong biblical emphasis.

She became interested in poetry at an early age as she participated in school and church functions, which consisted of recitations, speeches and drama. Later on, she began creating her own cards and writing verses for them, as well as, including poetry in her letters.

Over thirty years ago, when she was asked to work with the youth department in her church, Viola became increasingly more dissatisfied with the limited variety and the contents, which lacked motivation, in the resources that were available to work with at the time. This prompted her to create supplements to the available material, and eventually to write her own entirely. That has resulted in numerous inspirational writings, tributes, poetry, addresses, skits and plays.

Since 2005, Viola has published two other books: Check Yourself, which is a collection of inspirational poetry and Making the Right Choices, which is a collection of evangelistic drama for youth.

Her mission in life is to impact her world for eternity through sharing the Word of God. She believes that poetry is a means of capturing the attention of many, because it is easy reading, and it is viewed by many to be an expression of beauty; therefore, it paves the way for presenting truths that may otherwise be rejected.

Her church membership is with Gospel Temple Baptist Church in Luxora, Arkansas (Michael & Carol Mckinnie, pastors).

Questions or comments may be e-mailed to Viola at:

kingskid7438@sbcglobal.net

The Building Blocks to a Strong Marriage

Final Word

Even though long-term marriages are becoming obsolete, it is hoped that by taking this book to heart, it will open doors that have been locked by marital frustration, difficulties, or routine.

I believe that the majority of the issues that must be addressed for couples to work through their situations and develop a truly happy marriage, have been dealt with in this book. It takes a willingness to communicate, humility and help from God to be consistent in reaching that goal.

Every marriage, including my own, needs a checkup from time to time in order to continue maximizing a mutually satisfying life together as husband and wife.

When Adam was alone in the Garden, God provided him with a companion suitable for him to help him and brought her to him. When she decided to act independently of God and her husband by obeying Satan, the blame game was set into motion. And couples still use it today when marriages break up or break down.

That should not be, because God has given us back our dominion over Satan through Christ, and provision has been made for us not to give him any place of influence, expression or control.

The key is to "Trust in the Lord with all our heart and lean not to our own understanding and in all our ways acknowledge Him and He will direct our path." (Proverbs 3:5, 6, KJV)

Having an enduring, wonderful and thriving relationship with one's mate is an outgrowth of being rightly related to God through Jesus, who declared, "Without me you can do nothing." (John 15:5b) His making us whole, places us in position to not be selfish, demanding or insensitive.

It is impossible to have the kind of love that it takes for a couple to overcome all the difficulties or challenges that life presents, without a personal relationship with God. My reason for such an assertion is based upon what I have discovered in others who have successful marriages, as well as, what I've experienced in our marriage also.

God is love; love never fails--In order for a marriage not to fail, it must be rooted and grounded in love--for by Him all things are held together. (I John 4:8; I Cor. 13:8; Col. 1:17)

LaVergne, TN USA
06 February 2011

215400LV00002B/3/P